Until You Awake
Black And White Edition

SVC RECORDS

Until You Awake
A HYBRID MEMOIR-AUTOBIOGRAPHY
Stafon Von Camron

UNTIL YOU AWAKE: A HYBRID MEMOIR-AUTOBIOGRAPHY
Copyright © 2025 by Stafon Von Camron. All rights reserved. Printed in the United States of America. No part of this book may be used or reproduced in any manner whatsoever without written permission except in the case of brief quotations embodied in critical articles or reviews. This book is a work of non-fiction. This work presents factual information about real people, places, events, or ideas .

For information visit us online :
SVC Records | SVC Music Industry
http://www.stafon.co

Book and Cover design by Stafon Von Camron
ISBN: 9798898602246
Black And White Edition:

July 2025

10 9 8 7 6 5 4 3 2

All rights reserved. No part of this book may be reproduced by any mechanical, photographic, or electronic process, or in the form of a phonographic recording; nor may it be stored in a retrieval system, transmitted, or otherwise be copied for public or private use-other than for "fair use" as brief quotations embodied in articles and reviews-without prior written permission of the publisher. The intent of the author is only to offer information of a general nature to help you in your quest for emotional and spiritual well-being. In the event you use any of the information in this book for yourself, which is your constitutional right, the author and the publisher assume no responsibility for your actions.

Note:
This 6x9 hard cover, black and white book version which has less illustrations and photos. It of course lacks color too!

Until You Awake is also available in:
- 8.5 x 11 (full Color) Hardback
- 6 x 9 (full Color) Hardback
- 6x9 (black and white) Paperback
- Audio Book, DVD, Cassette, CD & Vinyl.

Purchase at: www.Stafon.co/bookstore.

CONTENTS

PREFACE 9
INTRODUCTION 11
CHAPTER ONE...................01
THE EARLY YEARS.
CHAPTER TWO..................05
GROWING UP.
CHAPTER THREE..............13
CHURCH AND FAITH.
CHAPTER FOUR................17
STOLEN CHILDHOOD.
CHAPTER FIVE..................43
ON MY OWN.
CHAPTER SIX....................47
THE END OF LIFE.
CHAPTER SEVEN...............65
GHOSTS AND SPIRITS.
CHAPTER EIGHT................87
LOSING WEIGHT.
CHAPTER NINE.................97
MEMORIES OF LIFE.
CHAPTER TEN....................100
HOLIDAY'S AND PETS.
CHAPTER ELEVEN.............130
A WORLD OF QUESTIONS.
ENDING 139
FINAL NOTE 140-141
ACKNOWLEDGMENT 144
ABOUT THE AUTHOR....146-147

PreFace

This book covers my life story, It is in a storybook fairytale style. With tons of illustrations and photos. It touches on child hood , physical and emotional abuse, angels, spirits, ghosts, relationships, family drama, unforeseen events, death, weight lose, world questions & theories and much more. Everything you need for a great book !

Introduction

I never kept a journal or diary. I figured that one day I would write my autobiography. This book goes from my birth up to the year 2025. If the average male human lifespan is that of 80, then I've already used up half of my life. I figured most people would have two autobiographies–one covering the first half of their lives and the other covering the second half of their lives.

I call this a hybrid memoir-autobiography, as it touches on my birth to the time of this recording. It's not in complete order, so buckle up and let's go for a ride. I talk about my feelings, what I thought, how different people affected my life, all the drama that will keep you thinking your family is normal after all.

In writing this memoir-autobiography about my life and those who affect it, I'm starting to see a pattern, which you might pick up on from chapter to chapter. I believe we never fully know ourselves as we are constantly searching for answers to who we are, how we act, why we do the things that we do, what is our purpose, and so forth. I feel like as we age, we learn a little bit more about ourselves. When you dive deep into your memories and start putting the puzzle pieces together, you can start to see how you become the you of today.

Note: Some full names of people living have been omitted or not fully exposed. Some places and names have been left out for privacy concerns. Some stories have been left out because some things are better left unsaid "Until You Awake."

Until You Awake
A HYBRID MEMOIR-AUTOBIOGRAPHY
Stafon Von Camron

CHAPTER ONE
The Early Years

I was born Stafon Von Camron in Tulsa, Oklahoma, on September 3rd, 1982. My parents were Susan and Cameron. My mother had just turned 16 in mid-March, so she was a young mother to me, which means we both grew up learning about the world. I also had a sister born three years later named Tana, who would later in life get married twice, going from a Holt to a Mouse. The moment I was born, you could tell that I was special.

Apparently, only one thing showed, as the rest would come in time. My mother had a few doctor visits before my birth. She said everything appeared fine in all of the ultrasounds. I was an active baby in her stomach—I was moving around a lot, or so she said. I was ready to get out! After I was born, the reason was pretty clear. The umbilical cord had wrapped around my left arm just below the elbow. In the doctors' and nurses' eyes, there appeared to be a worried look on their faces as they rushed me out of the room. Suddenly, my mother cried out, "Where is my baby, you fucking bitches! I want my baby now!"

I'm just surprised the nurses didn't say, "Oh my God, this girl is fully possessed like Regan MacNeil, who was possessed by a demon named Pazuzu in the 1973 horror film The Exorcist." So, with all of her screaming and acting like a wild animal in pain, you would think they would have been scared outright, but they must've been used to this kind of thing. After all, it was a painful childbirth. A nurse tried to calm her down, but my mother wasn't having any of it and ended up smacking the nurse across the face.

Apparently, the nurse was used to this type of behavior and just told her, "Are you done with your little hissy fit, missy? It's time that you start acting like an adult now," as the nurse injected some painkillers into her IV. My mother then finally calmed down, feeling the medication take effect. Like a child being scolded, she felt embarrassed—no one likes to be called out for their sudden wild outbursts. Then the nurse broke her thoughts: "So Susan, do you plan on keeping your baby?" My mother must have thought, "What kind of question is that?" as if they were playing "Papa Don't Preach" by Madonna in the hospital room next door.

The nurse then broke my mother's look of concern. To clarify her question, she said, "Susan, the reason why I'm asking this is because your son was born deformed, so you might not want him." My mother, with a sudden puzzled look on her face, replied, "What do you mean?!" in a startled but worried voice. "Well," the nurse said, "your son is missing an arm, so if you don't want him, we can put him up for adoption."

My mother, who was starting to feel her anger rise again, said, "I want to see my son first before I decide on anything so fucking insane!"

The nurse, who was tired of the cussing, said, "Susan, you need to calm down, or I'll wash your mouth out with soap." Like a mother reprimanding her child, this was a common practice in those days. My mother then told the nurse, "I'm sorry, it's just I'm upset and in pain. I just pushed out a watermelon-sized human body from my coochie, and it beeping hurts! I just want to know what the hell is going on here. Where is my baby? Let me see my baby!"

Then the nurse quietly said that she understood, as she walked into the next room to bring me back. Once my mother took a look at me, she said she looked past the arm and was instantly in love. I guess you could say that was the moment a mother bonded with her child.

My mother told me that the nurse made it seem like I was deformed or unnatural looking, and that she wouldn't want me. I'm assuming that was a common reaction they got to ask such a question, so it doesn't seem as strange now.

So, as the story goes, my mother decided to keep me, and from there on, my life would start in this crazy hell of a world that we now call home. I'm recalling most of these things from my memory or recalled moments that my mother or grandmother told me. I don't remember my toddler years in much detail—just little moments here and there. My memories that I do recall start around four years old. My mother had me fitted for my very first prosthetic arm through Shriners Hospital for Children. I remember we would take a bus to St. Louis. The drive there was long.

****

I remember seeing all the other kids in the hospital—some of them missing all limbs, some looking very deformed. It was at that moment that I remember thinking, "I can't complain because I could've been even much worse off." The thing about losing an arm is that you get used to it and adapt to everyday functions. You try to find a different approach to doing things.

The results come out the same or very similar. I feel like most of my life, I have used the "find a different way" approach to everything. I never wanted to be ordinary. I always had to find a creative way to do things. Let's just say I never followed a straight pathway.

So here I was, having this dead weight of a substitute arm strapped to me that I ended up hating so much. I decided I don't need this. I think at that point, it might have been the nosebleeds from popping my face with the hook, or just being a toddler who didn't like being strapped to a heavy apparatus. So from that point on, I did without it into my childhood and my adulthood.

CHAPTER TWO
Growing Up

My mother had to cut ties with my father by the time I was four. He was out of his mind from years of drug use and had tried to kill her by cutting her throat with a big kitchen knife. She said she had to use all of her strength just to push him off of her, as he was having a schizophrenic episode, seeing her as a demon that he needed to kill.

She said after that, she divorced him as he was locked up in an insane asylum for the mentally ill. She feared for us for years after that. Anytime they let him out, the word around was he came to town looking for us.

She had us hide out at the lake with our grandparents to protect us from getting kidnapped by him. When I was 15, I did go see him. The meeting didn't last long as he was living with his parents, whom—because of his past mistakes—had robbed a relationship of having a Grandpa Troy and a Grandma Jean around. At that point, they were all strangers to me and my sister.

The only memory I have of Troy and Jean is getting presents at Christmas from them by mail. Also, I remember them from visits to their travel trailer, where Jean would make me and my little sister breakfast while watching her favorite show, Jeopardy. I can still hear the timer music today from the show in my head.

Jean and Troy were truck drivers, so they lived a simple life at that point—they didn't need a big fancy home. Let me focus back on Cameron. So as you would've guessed, Cameron had another episode during my stay.

I was sleeping on the couch when suddenly I was awoken by a scared and out-of-his-mind Cameron. He was talking crazy gibberish that even at 15, I knew was not normal talk. He said things like, "They are after me," "They want to nail me to the cross"—he thought he was Jesus. I was tired, so I just fell back asleep, not realizing how serious the situation was. In the morning, Cameron was gone.

His parents, Jean and Troy, had him committed back into the insane asylum during the night. They got wind that same night that he wasn't taking his pills again. As an adult, I now think of how dangerous that could've been for me—had he had a knife, I would have been killed in my sleep, as I slept in the living room out in the open.

It was at that point I can say that my mother was absolutely right about the man whom I had known only as my sperm donor at that point. He was never anyone I knew. I never called him Dad, Daddy, or Father—he was always just Cameron to me, or what my mother would refer to as "Him."

Throughout the years, we would hear stories from his parents about him. They said he was put in jail for walking down the street in the nude, not knowing who he was, or that he was put in the insane ward after attempting to burn himself alive while burning down Troy's vintage travel trailer.

Years later, when it was discovered that Cameron had died and burned up in a house fire, it wasn't a surprise to anyone. The sad part is his dad Troy had died a few years before that of dementia, so he had no one to keep Cameron on close watch. Troy was the last one to keep him in line. Cameron had two brothers, so all three siblings grew up to be troublemakers, breaking the law.

Carl, who was the eldest brother, did settle down and seemed pretty sane, but his troubled past left him wheelchair-bound, and he died sometime before Troy. Ralph was the middle-aged brother—he died about a year after Troy. He was riding his motorcycle and somehow got killed running into a fence. When Cameron learned that he passed away, he tried to drown himself by riding his motorcycle into the lake. They had to put him in the ward again. Once he got out, they figured he still wasn't over losing all of his family, him being the last remaining family member. So they assumed he was again off of his pills and burned himself up alive like the past attempts.

The very last time I saw his mother Jean alive, was when my mother came to take me home, after finding out about Cameron's, so-called freakout. I remember she stayed for another day to visit and to catch up with them. I can recall that Jean and Troy were both fans of my music, as they were listening to my demo covers of Hank Williams on their CD player.

I remember Jean and my mother talking about her health. Jean was a heavy smoker, who ended up getting lung cancer.

I remember my mother telling her, to not give up as Jean had told her she didn't have much longer to live. Troy, let me drive his truck as I was getting close to the driver's permit age. That was a nice experience. I had many cousins on that side of the family growing up. I met up with my cousin Bubba during my stay. As kids we were close. Seeing him as a teenager was odd, I had some memory of him, but he had been around a bad batch of other teens, who drank, smoked, and had sex, so they all had lost their innocence.

I was only 15, but Troy would let me drive from his cabin to his mother's house, on the long dirt road, and would wave at Bubba walking along the road, as he looked impressed that I was driving. I was so cool, right? Years later, I would find out, that Bubba got into drugs from hanging out with the wrong people. At that point, there was no longer a connection to an old childhood friend. The past was left behind, so he was dead, so to speak and wasn't coming back.

I remember meeting Troy's mother, who as a kid, I knew as Granny Dye, oddly enough, this was right before she died. She had a little house with a big shed building behind it, that her son Don Senior used as a hangout hall, where all the bikers would hang out and have beer parties, things you might have seen in the early eighties. They had signs and everything, rock in roll and posters of hot naked women. I remember going to the creek nearby, building rock damns and watching the fish swim upstream with Bubba, Troy Junior and his older sister, Angelina, who was closer to mine and bubbas age.

Their father was Ralph, who was Cameron's brother. Like our family, they also had a bad relationship with their dad. He was in prison for most of their upbringing for killing a man in a bar fight. I was told that he beat up Cameron and bullied him every chance that he got, so he was a mean, angry person all of his life. I met up with Troy Junior during our high school days.

His mother had remarried, and Troy Junior had decided to take on his new stepfather's last name, which I hear Troy Senior was upset about. His mother said he was more focused on football and four-wheeling than he was on his studies. He grew up like me—no father around.

At least he got a stepfather that he must've liked to take on his last name. She said he was smart but seemed to not spell words correctly. He would write them out as they sounded. Troy Junior came home, we shook hands, but had nothing in common. If anything, he was more happy to take out his four-wheeler than to sit down with his first cousin.

His sister, Angelina, seemed more interested in talking with me. She said her brother was weird and probably doesn't remember me, since he was a few years younger than me and Bubba. Back in Arkansas, they all had motorcycles. Every time I hear a CCR song, it reminds me of Arkansas.

In Granny Dye's house, she had a hole in the floor that was covered, so anytime you stepped on that one spot, you could feel the floor giving away. She had an old-fashioned tea kettle that would toot out once it reached its boiling point. I remember she had an old-fashioned washing machine on her porch that had to be cranked by hand.

I can imagine the days when things were simple and people weren't as stressed out. It was a very different time then, even in the eighties. The last time my mother and I went to her house, her son Don and his wife had moved in and remodeled it into a log cabin. This was a year before Jean's death.

Since then, Bubba and his wife have lived there the last time we checked. The last time I saw Jean, I was attending her funeral. She had an open casket. I remember walking by it, looking down and feeling stunned that I had just seen her alive the year before that, but here before me was her body with no life. I signed the obituary guest book, as we left to go to the final site to bury her casket.

Lots of family from Cameron's side was there—they came over and told me how big I'd gotten, as many of them last saw me as a toddler. I only knew a handful of them. After the funeral, I walked out to my car only to find that I had a flat tire.

The good news is that Cameron was acting normal at that time and took me over to a local tire shop. He paid to replace my tire. I thought that was the most fatherly thing he could've done at the time. At the age of 16, that was the last time I saw Cameron alive.

I got to see Troy again when he came to my graduation back in 2002. That was the last time I saw him alive, however, my sister got to hang out with him right before he passed away.

STAFON VON CAMRON

Other than having a crazy sperm donor as a father, I grew up normal. Like most boys, I was into building mud pies and playing with sticks and stones, building little towns in the dirt, making little bug cemeteries with my friends.

I was also scared of catching cooties from girls. I had my yellow Tonka truck and my three-wheel bike that I would ride around like I was so cool.

My sister would be playing alongside me, making mud pies and role-playing as my student, as I would be the teacher, assigning her homework. I was a normal kid, or so I thought, up to that point, as things would start to get interesting....

CHAPTER THREE
Church And Faith

Our aunt Angie used to take us to her church on the move, which was mostly a tent revival or moved from building to building. It was an interesting gathering of Pentecostal people who would pass out or speak in tongues. The preacher was named Pat Quick. I remember admiring him because he was an adult and a man of God. I think everyone admired him, but also I remember he had a son around my age that I played with and thought was so lucky to have a father like him.

I remember one day Pat asked me to sing on the stage. I gladly took the mic from him and sang my favorite song at the time, "This Is the Day." Afterward, I remember him asking what I wanted to be when I grew up.

I think to satisfy him I said, "A preacher, just like you." In reality, I was thinking of a singer, of course. This seemed to make him happy. From that point on, I made it my mission to sing on stage every time I could, both at the tent and the church.

The part of the church that I found boring was all the preaching—weird, right? I guess kids have no interest in that or what they were even saying while reading from the Bible. Thank goodness for Bible school for us kids.

They always had us leave the room after the song service. We would all go to a room and watch puppet shows and watch little films about Jesus and how he died on the cross and all the things a kid would like in a cartoon. At the time, I was convinced that Jesus was a white man that spoke English.

I would find out later that the version shown before me was for children and my race and language. Imagine that Jesus was not white and spoke Hebrew—I wouldn't have understood or related to the cartoons, so I understand why churches all have their version of what Jesus looked like. Overall, my research on the Bible, I found out there are 26 different versions of the Bible. The most popular version is the King James Version.

I remember finding Pat's Bible. I found it interesting because it was in a "Bible for Dummies format" that was easy to understand. It was translated into modern English, so reading it, you understood the words and meaning so much clearer. I found it pretty clever. I just never understood all of the judgment people would put on other people just because they believed every line in a book that had been interpreted and rewritten many times throughout the years.

It would be many years later that I was awakened by religious fanatics who choose hate and judgment of others versus all-loving embracement of acceptance and love from a spirituality-based faith that is all-loving and accepting of everyone.

My relationship with God is that he loves and accepts me the way I am, as he made me and I'm a part of his grand plan. Years later, I would write a song called "What Would You Do?" God says, "If it's not from the heart, then it's not from me." This means that if it's not spoken from love, then it's not from me.

My Aunt Angie took me and, at the time, her three daughters to the lake. We were swimming in the swim zone. For some reason, Angie came over to me and lifted me, trying to pull my swim shorts down in front of her daughters. "How dare she try to expose me like that," I thought, as I held on to my shorts tightly.

To keep her from exposing me to her girls, who were all younger than me, I panicked and went on the attack. I reached down her bikini top as fast as I could and grabbed one of her breasts. It took her by surprise, as she gasped and dropped me right away.

I wasn't embarrassed at all, as my plan worked and none of them saw me exposed that day. I'm not even sure what my aunt thought about that, but I'm sure she learned a lesson that day. Do unto others, until it gets done to you.

I'm pretty sure my mother laughed about it when I told her. It wasn't a sexual thing—it was a "defend my integrity" type of thing. Of course, all my friends would want to know: How did they feel? Were they big? Did you like it? You know how boys are. Luckily for her, I didn't ever tell anyone other than my mother, who was the only one I would tell stuff to.

I saw my grandma Hitt less and less as she was busy taking care of her sick husband, who was known as Grandpa Hitt, who ended up dying in the year 2000. He seemed to have accepted me as a kid and even defended me when my mother didn't like the fact that I would walk around with a little pink Barbie purse full of pennies. Grandpa Hitt would say, He's just a kid, let him be."

I remember my mother secretly being happy when the purse was left in a restaurant. I cried losing my beloved pink purse. In her mind, she wanted a son who would grow up to be masculine, heterosexual, and strong.

CHAPTER FOUR
Stolen Childhood

I was over at one of my cousin's houses, from the other side of the family—the biker ones. My mother was there. She was busy with her friend who happened to be my second cousin. While her daughter was around 16, the age was old enough to babysit. I have a few horrible memories of being alone with her.

Both she and her sister did things behind their parents' backs, like driving their car to go to the lake and then sneaking the car back into the driveway before they got caught. My mother had left me with one of the daughters, and she took me to her room. I must've been around five. Old enough to know right from wrong. I remember she took off her clothes and had me on the bed next to her as she was touching herself.

She then grabbed my hand and put it in her vagina. I knew what she was doing was wrong, but she was older and bigger than me, and I didn't want to get into trouble.

I remember as she was using my hand to pleasure herself, I heard a knock on her locked bedroom door. It was my mother asking on the other side of the door, "What are you two up to?" The girl replied, "Just playing." I guess my mother had no other questions, as she left the hallway. There I was, left with this vagina wrapped around my hand and arm.

After I got out of the room, I went over to my grandma Hitt and confided in her to keep my secret. I told her about what had happened and told her "not to tell Mommy." Well, as you can guess, she did tell her. So now you may wonder, what did my mother do? Did she confront her or tell her mother? No.

My mother told me at the time she was just 21 and didn't want to lose her friend over it. If she were to tell her about her daughter molesting me, that would go bad and pretty fast. If someone told you that your kid molested their kid, who would you believe? I think at that point, my mother did not want to cause a scene and just kept it a secret. Did she let me around that girl anymore?

The answer is, hell no. She knew that was no longer a good idea and hid that fact well. The other times before the girl used my hand for pleasure was the time she would drag me around the room, pull me off the furniture, punch me, and beat me up as if, just because I was a boy, she could play rough with me, not knowing that she might've cracked my skull or hurt me badly.

The other daughter was older, and I never had issues with her. I guess she was more mature and a lot closer to my mother's age.

We encountered her again a few years later. She was impressed by how much I had grown, but her sister—the one who had molested me—showed up as well. She probably assumed I was too young to remember what she had done to me as a child, but those memories were deeply embedded in my mind I watched her in her bathing suit around my stepfather Steve, who was unaware of my childhood trauma.

I remember him commenting, "She's got a great body for having six kids." I wasn't surprised she had so many children. In my young mind, I saw her as a sexual predator who needed to fulfill her urges. This experience severely damaged my relationship with sexuality and intimacy.

As a teenager, I found myself drawn to certain physical attributes, but I also worried about my mother's romantic choices. My mother was strikingly beautiful—she resembled Pamela Anderson with her curves and long blonde hair. I often wondered why she didn't pursue the cosmetic surgery she frequently mentioned wanting.
"It's too expensive," she would say when I asked about breast implants.

Years later, when I brought it up again, her response had changed: "I'm too old now."
She procrastinated throughout her life and never followed through. "If Dolly Parton can have them at 70," I would tell her, "then you're never too old."

My mother went through what I called her "Britney Spears phase." She was obsessed with whitening her teeth until they were brilliantly white when she smiled. She maintained a flat stomach and wore a belly button ring, pairing it with low-rise jeans and crop tops—the fashion trend of the time when Britney Spears was at her peak popularity.

Mom was always beautiful. I constantly bragged about her to everyone. Her long, wavy blonde hair flowed past her waist and drew compliments wherever she went. It was heartbreaking to see such a wonderful woman tied to an alcoholic who made my life miserable.

Steve drank beer constantly and was consistently cruel to me. I remember one incident at his boss Larry's above-ground pool. He pointed to a spot in the water and said, "Do you see that?" As I leaned closer to look, the bastard pushed me into the pool, knowing I couldn't swim. Fortunately, I landed in the shallow end, but that incident deepened my growing resentment toward him.

You might wonder why I disliked my stepfather so intensely. To be honest, he didn't start out terrible. When my mother first met him, he seemed like a decent single guy living in a small RV at the campground next to our town's Walmart. The campground had rows of small trailers, and my mother brought my sister and me over to meet this new man she was dating. He offered us candy and cookies—whatever he could do to convince kids he was a good guy. Shortly after this introduction, my mother and he became serious enough to get married. That decision marked the end of our good times.

UNTIL YOU AWAKE

The wedding took place outdoors in a park. My mother had made her own wedding dress, and I was there while she sewed it. I even offered my advice when I noticed something wrong: "Mom, you're sewing the sleeves incorrectly!"

She dismissed me with, "I know what I'm doing."
I got the last laugh when she tried it on, only to discover she had sewn the sleeves together exactly as I had predicted. I must have been a designer in a past life, because I understood these things despite never having sewn anything myself. I think I learned by watching people work

The wedding seemed to go well initially. They had the reception at her sister's trailer, complete with a beautiful three-tier wedding cake. However, half of it was destroyed when my cousin Jennifer—who was always a troublemaker—knocked it off the table. She was such a brat back then, so I wasn't surprised. Perhaps that was an omen of the troubled marriage ahead.

As my mother settled into her new married life, we were able to move out of the trailer I had grown up in and into a small house set on twenty-eight wooded acres in the country. Her new husband Steve would bark orders: "Go out and bring some wood into the house," referring to the wood stove that heated our home.

****

I as freezing outside, and I remember my sister and me shivering as we gathered wood. He made us do this constantly while he chugged beer and belched and farted loudly. If you dared say no, he would stare you down with a look that suggested he might strangle you. It was genuinely terrifying.
He was extremely intimidating to children—even my cousins and close friends were scared of him.

I was jealous that they didn't have a mean stepfather like mine, though their mother was a religious fanatic at the time, so I was grateful my mother wasn't like that. Even though I found comfort in my mother, she let him control everything, and he ruined every good moment we might have had.

His cruelty extended to the smallest pleasures. If my sister and I were in the living room watching Saturday morning cartoons, he would storm in from the bedroom and change the channel to some boring football game or something else no kid would want to watch. He was being an asshole and he knew it. We would retreat to our mother's room to watch cartoons with her, but he would burst in almost immediately and tell us to "get the hell out." We never got to enjoy the simple pleasure of Saturday morning cartoons like most kids.

To compensate, my mother bought me a small black and white television set for my room. But even this small refuge was temporary. Steve would barge in while I was watching—he had removed the lock from my door—and turn off the TV without a word. Eventually, my little television disappeared one day, and no explanation was given. Her new husband Steve would bark orders: "Go out and bring some wood into the house," referring to the wood stove that heated our home.

You can see why I started to hate the man. He never acted like a father, let alone a good stepfather. His threats were vulgar and terrifying. He used to say, in his own charming way, "I'm going to rip off your head and shit down your throat if you don't do what I tell you to do."

One day stands out particularly in my memory. My mother was fighting with him—there was yelling, and then I heard a loud crash in the living room. When I went to investigate, I found my mother crying amid the shattered remains of our large glass piggy bank, with coins scattered everywhere. He had apparently thrown it at her. There were even holes punched through the sheetrock walls where his fists had connected.

I'm not sure where Steve was at that moment, but our mother loaded my sister and me into the car to leave. I finally thought, "Great, she's finally leaving his ass." My heart soared with hope. Unfortunately, after just a few minutes, she drove back to the house and decided to stay with him.

****

The Affair Years

My mother and Steve were growing apart. I think my mother was finally maturing and becoming more independent. After all, she was in her mid-twenties when she met Steve, who was twenty years older than her. She started having an affair with an older, wealthy man she met at work. Her reasoning was that she and Steve were divorced at the time, but since they still lived together, the relationship had to remain secret.

My mother's new sugar daddy treated her well, providing her money. Steve, however, was also having an affair with his best friend's wife, Linda—a busty woman who used to come over to swim in our pool.

Her breasts were always the center of attention, impossible to ignore. My mother knew about Steve's affair but didn't want to confront him since she was having one too. He even paid for my first little music album project, which made me like him for a while. However, after about a year, the drama began to unfold.

My mother's new sugar daddy treated her well, providing money and trips. He even paid for my first little music album project, which made me like him for a while. However, after about a year, the drama began to unfold.

He started living with my grandmother—my mother's mother—initially just as a roommate. As you might have guessed, being a man around an older widow who was lonely and hadn't been intimate in over ten years, things inevitably happened. The two began having sexual relations.

When my mother discovered this, she was furious at her mother for "stealing her man." She called it the ultimate betrayal. However, my mother has always been forgiving, so they eventually made up. She knew her mother hadn't done it intentionally. It's even possible he seduced her, as he was quite the charmer.

My mother wanted to cut ties with him completely, especially as he was becoming her stalker.

He started driving by our house several times a day, and she didn't want Steve to find out about any of it. She was terrified of what might happen if the two men ever met.

Her sugar daddy finally moved on to another younger woman, so my mother was free of him. Eventually, she found a man who was actually around her age. I think she finally got over her attraction to older men. After all, Steve was older than her mother, and her sugar daddy was around the same age as her mother. So it was a miracle that her new man was age-appropriate.

They had much more in common and could grow old together. Once Steve passed away, my mother could freely date without feeling guilty about it. She never really went through a "playing the field" phase. She was the type to cast her line and keep the very first fish she caught.

Fortunately, she did find herself a good man who respected both her and her children—someone who wasn't an alcoholic or drug user. That was a significant step up for her. Meanwhile, my sister's first marriage was falling apart, though she was completely oblivious to it. Most people had already figured out that her husband was a serial cheater who had been unfaithful throughout their entire eleven-year marriage.

In a way, she was lucky he was so incompetent. The guy was always running out of gas and lacked the common sense to fill up the car beforehand. My sister constantly had to rescue him with a gas can. This happened repeatedly.

After he left my sister, he had just had a new baby boy—his fifth child at the time, as he'd had a daughter with another woman before marrying my sister. I'm not sure if he has more kids now, but I wouldn't put it past him. I wrote the song "Oh Well" based on my sister's first marriage. She said it made her cry when she first heard it.

Currently, my sister has a new husband, and things seem to be going well for her. She's been able to watch her children grow up and experience the joys of motherhood. My sister and I are similar in many ways but also different. She grew up loving the same music I did. I think our exposure to various genres helped foster that shared passion for music.

I know I've branched off talking about my mother, sister, and grandmother, but these stories are part of my life, and people love this kind of drama. As a songwriter, it's excellent material to draw from. If you're a fan of good soap opera storylines, my family would keep you entertained with their tales.

****

One time I joked to my grandma that I was going to write a song about her being her own mother-in-law—only because she married her daughter's father-in-law. The marriage isn't by blood, but it does sound strange that her daughter is now married to her stepbrother. They had been married for nearly fifteen years before my grandma married his father.

At first, we told her, "Maybe you can date, but don't get married—that might be weird for your daughter." For a while, her daughter refused to talk to her, but I guess she got over it when she saw that her mother was happy. I get it—family drama isn't just focused on my own story. If anything, you'd want to see a TV show about our whole family's dysfunction on TLC.

Well, that's not going to happen. In recent years, my aunt and grandmother seem to be doing well with their husbands. My mother has her man, and my sister has her second husband. They all seem to be thriving.

But if you want to hear something truly weird, my aunt Angie started dating her cousin, which we all thought was bizarre. Apparently, they googled it and discovered that since he was a third cousin, they figured he was far enough out of the bloodline that it wasn't inappropriate.

Everything sounds absurd when you say, "My grandma is married to her son-in-law's father, and her daughter is dating her cousin." Like what the hell—is this Arkansas? Is it really that hard to find good prospects in these parts of the country?

The answer is apparently yes, given our family's track record of unconventional relationships. People always talk about "my soul mate this" and "my soul mate that." But I wonder—is your soul mate here on earth, or on the other side? I think they might be on the other side, because if they were here, why would so many people get married and divorced? Everyone seems to cycle through partners over the years, trading them in when they get worn out and need something new.

The thing you have to remember is that you're not getting any younger, so enjoy this moment today—tomorrow it will be gone.

CHAPTER FIVE
On My Own

I recorded my very first demo album in 2002 called "Miscible Voice," which means "can be mixed with." It was a fun scientific word that I thought sounded cool at the time, so I just tacked on the word "voice" to it. I wrote two songs for the album, with the rest being a mix of original songs by Lisa Marie Brennan and Jackie Worth, plus cover songs like "Another You," "Via Delarosa," and "El Shaddai."

Growing up, I was still singing in church, so when I discovered country music, I fell in love with it. My first memory of hearing country music was hearing Hank Williams sing "I'm So Lonesome I Could Cry" in the 1993 film The Beverly Hillbillies. He never appeared on camera, but his music filled the screen as Jim Varney danced around to the song. After that, I dove into Hank Williams and classic country.

Modern eighties country was my next discovery. I was outside listening to my mother's old beat-up tape player that had an FM radio dial on it. I had tuned into a country station, and the most beautiful song came on the radio that stopped me in my tracks. The song was called "Don't Close Your Eyes" by an artist named Keith Whitley.

I will say that song hooked me into being even more of a country singer. I even recorded a cover version of the song, using Keith as my vocal inspiration. I never thought, at the age of thirteen, I could be on the radio—I figured I would have to grow up first. Even though I thought that was impossible, I still used to have dreams of accepting a CMA award.

So here I was, this young boy wanting to be a country singer but feeling bummed that I had to be an adult to be a country star. That opinion changed when a young LeAnn Rimes took over all the news stations as this little girl with a big voice

I wanted what she had—a record deal, the records, the radio play, the fans. So I asked my mother to book and pay for a recording studio session for me to be a singing star. Of course, she didn't give me money—I had to earn it doing chores.

****

My mother was stingy with money. I think for my very first recording session, I had to pay the guy with quarters. How embarrassing! Not to mention my first demos were so bad I threw them away, but I still wanted to go back and try again. The problem was, I had no money, and after all, I was only thirteen—how could I work? To help me out, my mother arranged for people to pay me if I mowed their grass. That money was what paid for my thirty-dollar-an-hour recording sessions.

I remember when they played the film Sister Act on TV. I fell in love with the movie and wanted it—I think it was the music that stood out to me. At the time, VHS was popular, and I would see the film at the store for twenty dollars. My mother would not buy it for me. She said, "If you want that movie, you are going to have to earn it by saving up your allowance.

I was so annoyed, but I did want that movie so much. It took me months to save up twenty dollars to buy it. By that time, DVDs had started to come out, and there it was—Sister Act in a bigger new format with clear picture quality, but it was thirty dollars. You know I wanted it even more, but like before, I had to save up to buy it.

So you know how happy I was when I landed my first part-time job at the fast food joint Sonic, flipping burgers. This allowed me to pay for any recording session going forward without asking my mother for money.

I never understood why my mother was so tight with money. She was married to Steve at that point, who had a good job making expensive cars, so I'm not sure why. If it had been before Steve, then I could see why—a single mother with one income. I remember our choir class went to a song competition, and all the kids brought money so they could eat lunch at the McDonald's where the bus stopped. I was the only kid with no money to eat. I remember how embarrassing that was. It was like that until I got my first job.

Back to my independence. Even though I was moved away from home, I did see my mother at work. We both worked at a chicken plant at the time. I started working there my junior year of high school while still working at Sonic part-time. With work study, I was able to leave school after doing my one elective—choir—and my two mandatory classes: math and English. I did leave Sonic after I had enough money saved up to buy my first car.

I still kept the factory job because I was 18 and was already living on my own during my senior year. On my very first day on the job at the plant, the chicken guts made me throw up. I guess you could say I started getting used to the smell. I just know that at the time, it was good money having that job. I put in three years working there until I was fired by a mean and miserable-looking boss lady. She just saw me as a kid and didn't care that I had my bills to pay. She said I failed to clean the place up well enough, even though I was just placed on that crew. It was one of the highest-paid jobs in the chicken plant, but also the easiest one to get fired from.

I guess in a way, it ended up being a good thing. I was young and needed to do other things in life, so she pretty much did me a favor. How did I make it without money? Well, my sister was making money as a manager at Sonic and didn't want me to lose my trailer that I had been paying on for the past few years. She offered to move in and take over the payments while I focused on getting a real career, so I enrolled in beauty school.

I know you're probably asking yourself, "How in the world can he do that one-handed?" Well, so did the owners of the school, but I had thought of that even before I applied. I knew it involved my way of doing the job, and I was able to show them my way worked.

I used to tape a comb to my arm as an extension of my hand. This allowed me to do haircuts and roll perms—I had it down pretty well. I even upgraded from tape to elastic bands and then to customized pocket sleeves that I had my mother sew up for me. They allowed me to slip a comb in and out without using tape. To this day, I still use them.

****

I'm on the radio:

There was a local country radio station nearby. I had dropped off one of my CDs, and they played one of my songs on the radio! So I did get to experience my song on the radio at least once back then. I was so ready to be a star, but didn't know all the steps to take. I'm still bummed that I never tried to get a spot on the Grand Lake Opry. It was the next thing to the Grand Ole Opry, but in Oklahoma. I did sing at an outdoor jamboree stage with a real band as a teen a few times.

I also sang with a band named Renegade when they came to play at a 4th of July show at the wrong venue.
I would sing pretty much anywhere there was a live band. I had won a few talent shows, but also lost a few. Losing only makes you more determined to win.

STAFON VON CAMRON

I'm a model:

As a teenager, I was also wanting to be a male model. I noticed that I was getting pretty photogenic. I went to the John Ross Modeling Agency in Tulsa. The lady looked me over and said I had a good look. I think she referred me to a photographer they worked with. I was sent to follow this guy on his photo shoot session. There were five guy models around my age—stunning looking guys. He was having me shadow him, so he had taken them to the salon for haircuts and styles. The photographer had flown over from France to take their photos.

I knew I wasn't a part of the group, but the photographer was really asking me if he could take my picture too, so I guess I looked the part. However, I think the agent man told him I wasn't a part of that group just yet. I remember going back to the house with the models, and we were looking over all of the photos. They were picking the best ones. You know you have to take 100 photos to maybe get a few amazing photos. It all comes down to pose, look, lighting, and just the perfect moment. After that, I took several photos with all kinds of different male photographers.

I was signed to a few modeling agencies: John Ross, Linda Laymen, John Casablancas, and I & I Modeling and Talent Agency. I found out I was pretty photogenic in the face. They would say good for face work and maybe print and catalog, but they knew the arm thing was the only problem. So no runway or body modeling for me.

I think I just sat on the back burner of all those agencies—I never got jobs through them. I was only getting a few go-sees. I landed a lot of my gigs myself, including singing and modeling for catalogs. I was a determined guy in my 20s, so music was my next goal.

Back To Cosmetology School

After I got my license, I decided that I wanted to move to Tulsa, the city that I was born in. I ended up getting a great-paying job at SuperCuts. I was able to get myself a little apartment, and I was living my best life at the time. I was writing my songs with the help of a great guitarist and college professor who had charged me a fee to chart out my songs to sheet music. This was working well for me, and then I got discovered on MySpace.

I Got Discovered

A music manager had found my cover of "The Tin Man" on my MySpace page and wanted me to come to Florida for my artist development. I thought I was going to be a famous singer. It took some convincing, but I decided to follow my dreams and take the risk.

My mother gave me some money to move to Florida. I sold off everything I had and drove to Florida. It was promised to me that I would have a room, free food, and didn't have to work—I just needed to work on my music and get a backing band set up as I worked on my artist development. This, of course, was somewhat true. I arrived at the manager's house; he lived in a house close to the beach in a cove.

VERO BEACH FLORIDA

There were beautiful palm trees everywhere. I saw that it would rain a bit and then the sun would come back out. I loved Florida. I had noticed that even my allergies were gone and that winter was so mild and short compared to back in Oklahoma. I was greeted at the door by a tall, handsome-looking model who was another singer that was staying in the guest room, which was about to be mine. He was packing his bags to fly back to France. I was thinking, "Wow, this manager must be legit, or he could be a creepy old pimp daddy who lures in attractive guys on promises." I noticed right away that he was a heavy smoker.

As he puffed away on his cigar, he started to speak in a thick Italian New Jersey accent. He told me that he was an entertainment lawyer and represented and managed some big stars back in the '60s and '70s. He had lived in big, beautiful houses and had his own entertainment lawyer offices across several cities—he was what you call a big deal back in his day.

What I saw before my eyes was an old man in his mid-60s, still acting like the music industry would bow down at his feet. Looking at his list of clients, there were not any well-known younger artists. I just saw groups of bands from the '60s and '70s that may have had big hits. So I knew I was dealing with an old-school music manager, but at the time, I was just glad that he saw the talent and potential in me.

He then takes me on a tour of his small house and says, "This is your room. After you unpack your things, come out and we can talk about your music and career goals." The room was nice and clean, but I started seeing his strict rules almost right away. He said once you leave a room, you must turn off the lights.

I didn't pay any bills, so I assumed he just wanted a low electric bill. Being in Florida, they probably didn't need much light during the daytime. I would soon find out he was just a penny pincher. How can that make a good music manager? I stayed there six months. I was starting to get paranoid that he was a fraudster and upset because he wanted me to get a band, but he didn't want to pay anyone interested in joining it.

He wouldn't look into booking gigs until they knew all the songs and showed up to the non-paid rehearsals. Even when telling the guys that I was opening up for the Charlie Daniels Band, that still didn't make them want to play for free. These guys wanted money more than opening up for a country legend for free. He said, "If I can book you a gig, then you can get paid." So with that offer, of course, I couldn't get anyone to be in my backing band.

He often would lose his temper if I left a light on or listened to the TV too loud—little things that older people tend to get upset over. One night in November, he wanted me to have Thanksgiving dinner with him at the table. I didn't find eating with him all that important at all, and I thought it was an odd request. I just said, "No thanks." I don't know what he was expecting out of me, but I wasn't about to eat in front of him.

It was at that breaking point that he kicked me out of his house. Am I that bad for saying no? To you people with wondering minds, no—he was not having sexual relations with me. I was there for my music career and nothing else.

Life in Orlando:

Luckily for me, my uncle Clay and his wife lived in Orlando. I stayed with them for a few months while I saved up some of my paychecks from my new job at Walt Disney World. I would've done hair there, but I was still waiting on my hair license to transfer, which took a long time. I didn't like living there at the time, so it was just a temporary stay for me. It was a loud, stressful, uncomfortable environment for me. Plus, I didn't want to rely on anyone for help long-term, so I wanted out ASAP.

I managed to get a weekly stay hotel room. I was making just enough to afford it from my work at Disney. I did that for a while until one day, Mr. Manager calls and talks me into coming back to stay with him. He said he wouldn't yell at me or kick me out as he was just upset that day and lost his temper. I left my job at Disney to move back to his house. "What was I thinking? I was getting paid by Disney!" That ended up being just the same as before. He had lost his temper again, so I just packed up and left again, never to return.

I couldn't just go back to Disney that fast because there was a wait time limit on rehiring.

Luckily though, I had finally gotten my Florida hair license approved, so I was able to pick up a job the same day at Fantastic Sam's. I think I stayed at Clay's again for a few weeks until I had a few checks. I rented out my own space in someone's converted garage. It was also around the time I was looking for a band to sing with.

I'm a frontman:

I found a country band that was looking for a lead frontman, and I got the gig. It was called Harp's Band, and it was put together by a keyboardist named Leon Harp, who ended up being the biggest wolf in sheep's clothing.

He was also the local church's keyboardist. The man was probably in his mid-60s. Over half of the band members were older, but I looked past that because they were seasoned professionals. I learned all of the covers that they wanted to do. I gave them all the ones that I wanted to do, and we worked on the program list for an upcoming gig that Leon had booked.

Ripped off again:

The band was also interested in doing my original songs. I had written a few songs that Leon liked, and we had recorded both of them in the studio. I had paid for all of the sessions, but I only owed around $50 on the remaining studio bill.

I was waiting for the money from our first gig to pay for the masters and to pick up the recording sessions. Only to find out that Leon had beat me there and took all the master copies and made the guys at the studio delete everything. So he was the only one who had a copy of the recordings.

He refused to give me my recording sessions. I had written the songs, I had paid for everything, and yet this two-timing man of God thought he could get a huge paycheck from me by holding my master recordings hostage.

I had paid for all of the sessions and he wanted $30,000 from my music manager of all people before he would return my stolen music to me. Leon's demands were only laughed at by my music manager. He said, "Leon isn't getting any money from me or you. You are not even a big selling artist—if anything, you're an unsigned broke artist." He also said, "There was no use suing Leon because he surely didn't have any money either."

I already had all of my songs copyrighted with the Library of Congress the year before, so I knew Leon couldn't do anything with my songs, or he would be toast. My songs were already protected, but Leon had my masters. If Leon released them, he would be sued for sure. Also, years later, I have written much better songs, so I'm shocked my early attempts were stolen.

The thing that upset me the most is the time and work I put into those songs. I worked to pay for the recording sessions, Which for two songs cost around $1,000. So when Leon kidnapped my music recordings, it was like someone taking away something that I worked very hard for. I had never had a live band in the recording studio playing my songs before, so the fact that he took those recordings from me left me devastated. So as you can guess, I left his band.

After all the musicians found out about what he did, some of them also left. However, some stayed on as spies for Leon—like two-timing double agents, so to speak. Who can you trust nowadays? I was starting to learn the dark side of people and the music industry.

Pete had told me that the singer they replaced me with was horrible and that he preferred playing with my group instead. Another time he said Leon wanted me back in his band, as he had fired the replacement singer.

I said to Pete, "No way. After what Leon did to me by stealing my masters, I was done with him, period." He must've thought his arrangements of my songs were gold records. I guess he forgets that I filmed the whole recording session for a video I wanted to do for the behind-the-scenes, so I had footage of them playing one of the songs in full.

The goal for me was to do more studio work and stage gigs. However, all we ever did were some jam sessions, and nothing came out of it. I do have video footage that I recorded—we tried to do different versions of my stolen songs. We did covers in many styles. It was always fun, but never seemed to go anywhere. Even though my band didn't take off, I had befriended a keyboardist named David.

That ended up being a good thing—I learned how to play the piano there. He had a baby grand piano and lots of keyboards and organs. He was classically trained on the piano and worked selling baby grand pianos at a music store in Orlando. I took up online classes from videos on YouTube. I learned how to chord notes in only two months. I was then able to play and chart my original music. From then on, I wrote so many songs after that.

I felt like that was a blessing and the right path for me. I think being around all the pianos helped kick my butt into learning how to play one.

Always on the move:

I moved around several times after that. I rented rooms in houses and shared spaces. I was there for three years and still felt like I hadn't grown any new roots to settle down. Maybe I was just homesick.

My mother would call me up and say, "Your grandma is getting older, and your sister's kids are growing up without their uncle around. You're a stranger to them." If she was trying to get me to come back, she was doing a good job.

I finally did decide to leave Florida. I had tried and tried to make it there with music, bands, recording studios, and jobs, but nothing ever seemed to work out. I was feeling hopeless, and I left Florida feeling defeated, which ended up being a dumb thing to do. Had I stayed, it might have been a good thing. Of course, now I'll never know. Don't get me wrong—it was only one of many paths that I could have taken, but was it the right one?

Back to Oklahoma:

I stayed with my mother, only because Steve had passed away. All the years of drinking finally did him in. I would love to say he was gone, but he wasn't, so to speak. He still messed with me in other ways after he died. My mother wanted me to babysit her house while she was out of town, but she failed to tell me that Steve was haunting her house.

I will go into more details about that in another chapter, but for now, I needed to focus on my next move, so I went back to beauty college to get my master's instructor license. It took about four months, then I graduated, got my newest hair license, and moved back to Tulsa.

I had to get away from that house and the memories of Steve and, of course, his ghost.

Back to Tulsa:

When I moved to Tulsa, I tried to recreate the same setup as in Orlando—to set up a country backing band. We had a few jam sessions, but everything would just fall apart due to scheduling, and there were no places to play in Oklahoma. Most of the guys were not up for traveling for gigs.

So I made the decision to just deal with studio musicians and do music demos instead. I would have professional tracks to sing to, would be able to only worry about myself, and didn't have to worry about who is or isn't going to show up to play the music live.

Some kind of trouble:

I did a few demos with an older pastor musician. You would think I would stay away from the Christian god-loving type people, as they seem to be trouble, but I gave this guy a chance. This guy played a lot of instruments on the side. He even gave guitar lessons to people. He had a home studio set up in his basement, so I would pay him to record a handful of my song demos with him.

He did a good job. He would do the drums, bass, and guitar and craft a track that matched my chord chart and song melody. I would do the vocals, and then I'd have a semi-professional demo for not much money to take to Nashville to re-record with the big guns.

So I had set my sights on going to Nashville next. What would await me? More drama? Or like Tanya Tucker would say, "Some Kind of Trouble."

CHAPTER SIX
The End Of Life

It was the year 2020. People were freaking out because COVID-19 was spreading fast and killing a lot of people. We feared that it was the end of life. Many of us stayed at home, counting the days away and hoping that we weren't next on death's checklist. Some people found themselves with more time on their hands, and this forced them to take a good look at their lives and look at what was important to them, as it could all be taken away at any moment.

I was working at a fast food joint, and I was planning on opening up my very first salon. It was something that I was serious about; however, those plans got put on hold for another two years. Once COVID-19 started to spread, all of us were taken off of the work schedule, other than the managers—unlucky them.

I signed up for unemployment benefits that same day. I was able to still bring in a paycheck every week. The government also sent out a $600 a week booster check on top of our unemployment payments, which made so many people super happy.

STAFON VON CAMRON

Imagine getting $1,000 a week just to stay home because you were forced not to work during a deadly outbreak of COVID-19. Most people weren't allowed to go anywhere but outside in wide open spaces. People spent time six feet apart in large outdoor spaces like parks. Some people just stayed home and shopped online.

During that time, I was ordering things for my salon that I wanted to open up and was also paying all my bills off. So I was investing in my future. I also thought, "If it's the end of life as we know it, why not try to follow my dreams if time was running out?" So I found a producer in Nashville and started working on my very first professional country record. "It's about damn time!" I would tell myself.

I went to Nashville for the very first time in July of 2020. I met all of the studio musicians—they were all A-grade players, which means you got people who played on famous albums by Taylor Swift, Dolly Parton, Garth Brooks, Reba McEntire, Alan Jackson, Randy Travis, etc. Before they started the session, the producer asked me, "What kind of sound do you want?" I told him, "I just really wanted a '90s country sound." He looked over at John King and said, This guy is the king of the '90s country sound." John said that he was able to set up a good life after working with Reba and Garth, so I was in good hands with the best. Well, I watched them track my first song, "Oh Well."

As they play along, I hear a voice say, "Does that sound good to you, Stafon?" The studio engineer asked me. "Yes, it does," I would say. I knew nothing about the Nashville song-making process. I just relied on them making the best track out of my demo and song chart that I had sent. They got everything how I wanted—the melody, the key, the type of style I wanted.

They wanted me to give them a vocal guide track to follow, so I stepped in the vocal booth and sang along as they played my song so that they could get the right feel and timing that was needed to create the final recording. A vocal guide track is just a fast sing-through—it's something that they use to construct the music behind the voice before the actual song vocals get recorded. You may also hear it referred to as a guide vocal.

After recording my very first music track at the Watershed Studio in Nashville, I then follow the producer as we drove over to Hilltop Studios to record the lead vocals. They weren't lying when they called it Hilltop, as the recording studio was on the top of the hill.

Hilltop Studios is Nashville's longest continually operating studio. Built in 1963, it recorded such legends as Johnny Cash, Dolly Parton, Loretta Lynn, and Merle Haggard, just to name a few. We went into Studio A, and he was telling me about all of the people that had recorded there. They had photos up on the wall too.

The spot I sat on the couch, which I was unaware of at the time, was the same spot that Dolly Parton had sat just a few days before. Can you believe that I was in the same studio that so many greats recorded in? There was a huge number of country stars that had been there to record. So it was a neat moment for me. I go to the vocal room, where there is a studio microphone hanging from the ceiling in front of a big, massive glass window, where you can see the sound engineer in front of a big two-way split sound mixing board that is around eight feet long.

I was standing in the same spot that every modern country star—Lainey Wilson, Doug Stone, Vince Gill, Alan Jackson, and Tracy Lawrence—had stood to lay down their vocals.

I was so tired and worn out after staying up all day. I had a long drive ahead of me, even before they recorded my track. Another client had booked 10 tracks before me. I had to sit through it, so it took all day before it was finally time to do my track. I knew I wouldn't be at my peak recording voice, as I was tired and weak from lack of sleep, so I told him that laying down the final vocals on the whole album would be better for me at another time.

I wouldn't be at my peak recording voice, as I was tired and weak from lack of sleep, so I told him that laying down the final vocals on the whole album would be better for me at another time.

I mostly told him this because I was tired—my voice was sounding weak. I could also tell that he had no idea how to mix vocals, just from watching him mix the guy's vocals before me. So I was thinking, "This guy thinks he's a producer. He sits in the chair and says, 'Okay boys, play.' That was pretty much it." When all the studio players did all the work, it was clear he wasn't a good engineer. He just had good connections.

UNTIL YOU AWAKE

So I had planned to come back to Nashville once all my tracks were done to lay down the vocals with an actual award-winning sound engineer. I ended up using a local studio in Tulsa to lay down all the guide vocals to make sure the current music tracks would fit my voice. Out of the 14 tracks that they made for me, only 12 were finished and somehow worked for me. However, there was no one to make adjustments to the tracks as he sent no stems to remix. Let me go into a bit more detail.

So I'm on Facebook, and I see this ad for "Grade A studio musicians in Nashville. Your songs radio ready, call now." Let me remind you, it's 2020—people thought it was the end of life for them, so of course, if you can do it now, then you better do it now was the feeling that everyone had. So because I wanted to be a country star, I called. I spoke with a man who said he was a producer. I told him that I was a singer-songwriter and that I wanted to release a polished-sounding country record from out of Nashville. He talks me into trying out one song first to see how it goes.

I agree to pay him $1,000 for the recording session. Kinda high for just one song, I thought, but he said, "It's because you are getting pickers like John King, who played on hits for Garth and Reba, and Wanda Vick, who played on hits by Taylor Swift, among others." So I agreed to try it.

We arranged the studio date. Before I would drive down, I would send in my song chart with the song lyrics and chords, along with a video of me playing the song on the piano, singing the lyrics and melody how I wanted. He would then send it to the studio musicians before the recording session. The day arrives. I started off driving the night before, as the drive was around 8.5 hours and I had to be there in the morning.

I arrived at the Watershed Studio in Nashville as the studio players got there, walking into the building one by one. I waited for the producer to get there before I went in. I'm pretty shy, so you know, I was uneasy for a bit.

Everyone had to wear face masks, as COVID-19 was rapid. Everyone sat far apart in the room as the producer played them the rough demo I sent. They all listened to it—I guess this is a way to remind them of which song they are tracking today and how they are going to play it, as they did 10 songs before getting to mine. I can imagine some might have fiddled around with it at home before coming in, or maybe just winging it on the spot by hearing it for the very first time.

I'm not sure what their method was, as each person does things differently. They all go into the recording room. They were all recorded at the same time, almost like a live band rehearsal. Then they would record one at a time separately once they had a drum track and bass line to play to. They were able to fine-tune what they wanted to do.

This is also the time they need a scratch vocal to get the most out of the track and to make sure they were making the song sound like how I wanted it to sound. So I would get in the vocal booth and sing the song along with them live. Then they go back to listen and adjust their playing to fit the melody correctly.

Finally, the track was finished, and everyone was satisfied. The producer then wants me to go over to Hilltop Studios with him to record a studio vocal. I felt like he did nothing leading up to this—they were the ones who put the song together and did all the work, but he was the guy that I was dealing with on this project.

Before Nashville:

The unemployment and the booster checks came to an end after just six months. It was time to go back to work. It still wasn't safe. People were required to stay six feet apart, wear a face mask, and get a COVID vaccine shot, or possibly be fired.

Most people felt forced to do this because how else could they live without an income? Some people revolted and refused to take the vaccine, not knowing what the side effects would be years down the road. The one-shot rule turned into two shots, and then three, and then so on. I only got the first two.

I waited for almost a full year to make sure it was safe, as there were reports of healthy people dying from taking the vaccine. After finding out that the shot didn't stop COVID-19, it was no longer needed for me anymore. No matter how hard anyone tried to prevent getting COVID, it still would find them.

No matter how many years or months you went without catching it, it would still get you. COVID-19 affected people differently. Some got so sick that it killed them. Others had issues with smelling and tasting that would last months at a time, or they had lung and breathing issues.

Then you had the mild version that only seemed like bad allergies, but much worse. It was doing major damage to sensory nerves, killing them off.

I was working cutting hair at a name-brand hair salon, and people came in swearing they just had allergies. There was no way to test yourself because COVID-19 tests were hard to get—many stores were sold out, and doctors' offices weren't wasting tests on everyone. had developed this strong, feather-like tickle, so every time I talked or felt any vibrations, I would cough as a reflex. I did have COVID, according to the doctor I saw.

It attacked the sensory nerves in the back of the throat, so any vibrations at all would cause you to cough. Now, imagine coughing a thousand times a day. That causes the vocal folds to slap each other constantly to the point that they get damaged.

As a singer, it's the worst thing that can happen. The doctor said it attacked and killed off the sensory nerves. The good thing about sensory nerves is they regenerate; however, the process takes six months to a year. The first time I got COVID, it damaged my voice for six months before I could sing a note on key and talk without my voice cracking. Since this was after my Nashville trip, I already had all my music tracks created but hadn't recorded and finalized the vocals yet.

So this would throw a big wrench into my plans. Back to Nashville: After I got home from Nashville, I had planned to go back once all 15 song tracks were completed, where all the final mixing and vocals would be mixed and finalized. Until then, I relied on doing everything over the internet. When he offered a price reduction if I bundled more than one song at a time into a so-called piggyback recording session, I would save money.

No response. Cut off cold turkey. I started to feel like I got scammed. I had to leave them a one-star review under his business on Google to warn others about it. I also think after the first four songs, he hired cheaper players because the quality of the studio players was sounding cheaper. Here I was with unmixed tracks, no vocals, no stems, and no way to adjust the instruments or remove them. I was stuck with what was provided, so there was no way to make the tracks sound better. Also, there was no way I could afford to get them redone. I was forced to just use them as they were, in a crappy demo-like mix.

The tracks weren't the best mixed, but they were just okay. Too loud in some spots, too soft in others, with instruments I didn't like and organ sounds that I wasn't into. Since the producer wouldn't reply to me to set up a new recording session, I had to record my vocals in Tulsa. The sound engineer did his best to adjust the backing track volume, but he couldn't do much since he had no stems.

So at that point, I was just singing to overpriced karaoke tracks. Out of the 14 tracks, I got 12 that were somewhat usable. I had to pull out some old demos to fill my album with 15 songs. The Nashville producer, who also was a pastor at his church, was used to bringing in lots of money. I researched the guy—apparently he was in prison for fraud and cons, defrauding people out of money. So again, here he is still doing it under the guise of a Christian pastor who also produces both country and Christian music in Nashville. He has so many people fooled. It's sick that people do this to other people.

My one-star review got other people reaching out to me about what he had done to them. They said the same thing: "At first the tracks were great, then they started getting crappy tracks, unfinished tracks, and then none at all." He had stopped replying to them as well. A few even told me they were suing him in small claims court to get their money back. I thought about that, but being in another state, I wasn't sure how it was done or how to do it. I was told if I sued him in my state, he would be forced to come here to court or be found guilty.

Why does this keep happening to me?
Why do so many people take advantage of me and other people?
Do they sense weakness, or can they just smell a sucker from miles away that they can rob?

****

A Mini Chapter:

Back when I was in high school, I wanted to see how my classmates would respond to one of my cover demos. So during our senior prom, I had rented a beautiful black tuxedo with a long, feather-like split in the back—very nice looking, simple but beautiful. I had brought my demo with me on a CD. I went up to the DJ and asked him if he could play my demo, but not to let anyone know it was me. I was dancing with the valedictorian of my class. When I heard my recording come on, it was a cover of "Another You," a song written by Brad Paisley and originally released and recorded by David Kersh. I sounded great, so I told her it was me singing, but I don't think she believed me.

It was only after the end of the song that the name of the singer was exposed. The DJ yells over the microphone, "And that, ladies and gentlemen, was your very own classmate," as he says my name.

I wasn't expecting that, but it did sound amazing to hear my voice come through those big, expensive speakers. People seemed surprised that it was me singing, and I had a full line of people come over, one at a time, to tell me they loved it and encouraged me to go for a music career, so it ended up being a great night.

Getting applause and approval from my school classmates meant I was now ready to go pro. My prom date was a girl that I agreed to take to the prom. Her mother was a friend of my mother's, and they had worked together, so they set it up.

The girl, of course, had other plans on her mind. Once she'd gone to the prom, she'd secretly have her boyfriend meet her there in the parking lot so she could run off with him and go to the lake so they could have sex, all behind her mother's back.

Talk about rude, shady, and sneaky. Other than that, I wasn't upset or worried about it. I didn't know the girl, but she did like my suit. I just know that I went home alone back to my trailer house, happy with how my song sounded out loud and sure of the path I wanted to take.

Other Nashville Producer:

So, before I was conned with the whole album payout, I had run into a website of a company in Nashville that produced high-quality demos. His prices were fair, so I agreed to do two songs with him.

Out of the two that they did for me, I liked one better than the other. I did have it redone the first time—I told him I hated the organ sound, so I told him to replace it with a banjo, and he did. Made it sound so much better.

I added that song to my album. Even though the other guy recorded another version of the song, I think I preferred the classic-sounding version over the modern-sounding one. Both were on my "Oh Well" album. I called the songs "Windmill (Classic)" and "Windmill (Modern)."

So out of four producers I spoke with in Nashville, I worked with two in total at different times. I think the only difference was that the first one was a real producer but didn't use A-grade studio players.

The other producer was a con artist who charged higher prices but had connections to A-grade studio players. So that was the difference. I'm sure he took a bigger fee than what he was paying them.

STAFON VON CAMRON

The Aftermath:

So, because I was excited about my first album, I released about 50 of them on CD. I named the album after one of my songs, "The Star of the Show." The packaging was okay-looking, and the vocals were recorded at Drape Studios in Tulsa; however, I wanted to redo all the vocals, as I had more time to decide what I wanted to do differently on how I hit a note or how I sang a word. So I set up a new session at a different studio and booked three days so I could record new vocals on 15 songs.

After that, that same studio also did professional-looking music videos at $500 a pop, so I was talked into doing three music videos. We did two on the same day. I went to a cemetery to do "I Cry Myself Tonight," and then we drove out to the country to record footage for "Gone With the Wind." In both videos, I was 160 pounds. I was on a diet, losing weight. My goal was to get down to 140 pounds. Looking back at those videos, I still had a little bit of a stomach.

By the time we did the third music video of the title album track, "Oh Well," I had reached my goal of 140 pounds. I also changed up my look from a clean-shaven face to a big black mustache, so I almost looked like someone else, but of course, it was still me. After that video, I went back to being clean-shaven. I wanted to do more music videos, but it added up when you have bills, so I had to take a break from videos.

Off Random Memory:

It was wintertime. Snow was on the ground. Mother, my sister, and I got a sled and would take turns riding down the big hill, or hollow, behind the house. It was a large hill. My mother had brought her VHS camcorder to record it for memories.

I would say I was around 10 and my sister was around 7. My mother put the camera on top of the hill and pointed it to record the fun. I watched my sister and mother go down the hill in the sled several times.

Then, it was my turn to ride down with my mother. I sat in front. As we went down the hill, the sled went off course and was heading straight toward a tree. We were going super fast, so we were heading toward an impact.

My mother put her arm in front of my head just as we hit the tree, which honestly probably saved my life. Head trauma is a serious thing, so an impact on a tree could be deadly. The G-force of it knocked me off the sled and knocked the wind out of me.

I could be seen getting up, moaning and saying that I couldn't breathe. All the while, my mother hit the tree directly, almost wrapping her whole body around it. She was worse off for sure, as you could hear her moans of pain. She then yelled out to my sister to call 911 for help. I finally got my breath back—luckily I wasn't hurt.

My sister was already at the top of the hill, so she ran to the house. In the video, you can hear her slipping on the icy porch, letting out a loud cry. She was crying because she hurt herself while she was still on her way to call 911. I made my way up the hill moments later and saw the camera. I got in front of it like a news reporter doing an on-the-scene live broadcast and said, "My mother fell down and broke her hip," as I made a slight giggle. I think at that moment, I figured she would be fine.

I was just too young to think that it could've killed her. The emergency responders made their way down the hill with a handheld gurney. At first, they had issues getting it to expand because of the extreme cold weather and carrying her up the steep hill, as it was covered in snow, but they finally were able to load my mother up and get her to the hospital.

She ended up not breaking any bones, just badly bruised. There may have been some internal damage done, but I was still too young to remember the whole outcome. Let's just say she is alive and well at this moment anyway. For some reason, if you went back and watched the video, it was pretty intense seeing us smack the tree so hard—like a moment you want to play over and over on repeat, seeing it all unfold live on tape.

It was like one of those rare real-life accidents that happened to be caught on camera, where it's real and intense, but it was also followed by a funny moment after a serious moment. For years, people came over just to watch the tape. It was like the perfect horror moment mixed in with the perfect funny moment, all caught on VHS tape. People would say, "You should send it in to America's Funniest Home Videos—you would win!"

Since that was the only copy, it was stolen by, possibly, my stepdad's daughter Amber and her boyfriend at the time. So there is no telling where it's at now, or if they destroyed it or just cashed it in somewhere. It was that impressive—people saw a golden moment on tape, like lightning in a bottle kind of moment. The technology was on a home VHS tape, so it's probably not playable now or has degraded over the years, but let me tell you, it was quite a moment caught on tape.

Golden moment on tape, like lightning in a bottle kind of moment. The technology was on a home VHS tape, so it's probably not playable now or has degraded over the years, but let me tell you, it was quite a moment caught on tape.

It's a shame that home digital cameras weren't around then or that we didn't have a way to copy it to the computer. I had some other funny moments of mine on VHS tape that are gone as well. I was a funny kid and always had something to say. There was another time when Amber and I were home alone, listening to Michael Jackson's hit song "Black or White." As the camera was on me, I somehow did the moonwalk for a slight moment—it was so cool to see on the video. I didn't even know how I did it.

The funny part, though, was I was role-playing with Amber, so I grabbed a picture of Steve and held it up like he was talking to her toward the camera. I mocked his voice as best as I could: "What are you doing, Amber? Go clean your room, or I'll rip off your head and shit down your throat!" She just laughed out loud because I got it spot-on—that is how he would talk and what he would say. I remember my mother saw the video and thought it was funny. I was worried about Steve seeing it.

I don't think he ever did, or so I hope he didn't. That tape and the snow sled one both just disappeared. They were great home videos. If you ever find them, please digitize them and send them our way. Other than that, the memory is still there.

Back to My Album:

After redoing the vocals and doing music videos, I released the "Oh Well" album on 1,000 replicated CDs, 100 cassette tapes, and 500 vinyl records. I was serious about it. Such a long dream finally came true. It was also on all the online music stores and streaming platforms. I guess I overdid it a little. I had no idea how much space 1,000 CDs and 500 records would take up and how hard it would be to sell physical media in 2024.

My next country and pop albums would sound so much better when I took over every aspect of album making, getting better at being my own producer and sound engineer by using GarageBand, AI mastering, and other professional tools of the trade to create my custom-sounding demos the way I wanted. I plan on doing music as long as I can, going down my dream checklist.

No matter what anyone says, do what you want to do and make yourself fulfilled. If you can't get it done on a larger scale, then try it on a smaller scale. Just doing it is the reward. I may not be a big artist, but I'm still doing what I love. After all, we all have our hobbies, talents, and passions. Without them, this would be an even duller place to live out our lives, with death being the final reward and escape that we get.

CHAPTER SEVEN
Ghosts And Spirits

It was the year 2000. I was a sophomore in high school. The family was all at the local hospital because Grandpa Hitt was dying. We all were standing around his bed as he was taking his last breath. I noticed that he reached his hand toward the ceiling, as if he was reaching out for someone's hand.

You couldn't see anyone, but he could. I believe that a loved one from his past, or even an angel, came to take him to the other side. The moment he grabbed at the invisible hand, his spirit left his body, his arm fell back down on the bed, and his vital signs went flat.

He was no longer with us. I had cried all my tears out that day at the hospital. He had been the only grandpa that I knew at that point. Because Grandpa Hitt was a war veteran, he was buried in Fort Gibson, Oklahoma, at the memorial cemetery.

They had soldiers lined up to carry his casket. They presented my grandma with a folded American flag in a triangle wooden display case with a glass front. I remember some family members crying as the shotgun salutes went off.

I had done all my crying back at the hospital, so by the time we buried him, I had no tears left. I believe he had gone home and was finally at peace after seeing with my own eyes at the hospital that he was taking someone's hand from the spirit realm. This was the first time that I was connected to life after death.

As a teenager, I used to dream about flying. I would jump up in the air in my dream, with a feeling of floating, and I was able to stay up in the air for a long time, almost like air gliding. It seemed so real to me.

It would happen so often that I almost believed it was something that I really could do. It never occurred to me that it was happening not in a physical way, but in a spiritual way. I would be in a deep sleep dreaming. You know the type of dream where you're walking on the top of a 100-story skyscraper, and you somehow fall off?

Well, most people seem to jolt awake right before they hit the sidewalk. I always heard that if you don't wake up before you hit the sidewalk, then you can die in your sleep. I think that's why people were so scared of the Freddy Krueger films. Dying in real life from your dreams would freak people out.

Well, anyway, I would be sleeping, maybe dreaming of flying, when all of a sudden, I would just wake up. Only for a split second, I could feel my body levitating before I would feel my weight come crashing back down onto the bed. I could feel the bounce even—almost like bouncing on a mattress. Was I floating? Was I dreaming of falling and my body jolted awake out of shock and felt like it was real? Almost like Neo getting disconnected from the Matrix, from the wired socket in the back of his head.

I have my theory on it:

I believe that it was my soul returning into my body at that same moment. Some believe that as we dream, our souls leave our bodies, and we roam around free from our physical bodies, but we return to our bodies before we wake up. Some people have said they have woken up not being able to move. I read that this happens when they wake up before their soul returns.

I had never had this happen before, but as a teenager, I was always waking up to my body feeling like it just fell on the bed from levitating. That happened a lot then; as an adult, however, it never happens anymore. Upon my research, some have said they would wake up frozen in fear, seeing a demon, or a succubus, or something otherworldly sitting on top of their chest, trying to seduce them, as they couldn't move or speak.

Granted, this sounds crazy, right? A succubus is a female demon in folklore that is believed to visit men in their sleep to have sexual intercourse. The male equivalent is an incubus. Succubi are often depicted as beautiful women with the ability to seduce men, and their actions are often linked to causing male health problems and even death.

I never had this happen to me before. I guess because my positive persona blocks out any negative energy, or at least I try to keep negative energy away from me. They say that darkness is attracted to light, so that might be why I get so many crooks that try to take advantage of me.

UNTIL YOU AWAKE

Even from a handful of weird things happening to me, this has opened me to the fact that, yes, there is something more out there. It was late at night. I was at home alone in my apartment in Tulsa. The front door was locked, and my bedroom door was locked. Living in the city, I always took precautions. The only light coming into the room was the glare of the moon or maybe a street lamp that was glowing on the closed window blinds.

I was in a deep sleep, so I was shocked that I was suddenly awoken by the feeling that someone, or something, was standing right next to me. It's like a sixth sense that you get sometimes. I've never had that kind of sensation in a deep sleep before. I'm pretty sure that I was in the REM state of sleep at that point. Anyway, I opened my eyes to see this lady looking down at me. She was standing right next to the bed. Of course, I was startled because I was supposed to be safe behind two locked doors. So how could someone get in?

I was she trying to murder me in my sleep, I thought. So out of reflex, I swung my arm out to hit her! It was only a reflex, kind of like when someone jumps out in front of you and scares you, so you might just punch them in the face. This lady was standing by my bed in a long blue dress —she had long dark hair.

Honestly, the moment happened so fast that I can't give you much more detail on what she looked like. I just know I didn't know who she was, why she was there, or how she'd gotten into my locked apartment.

Those were the questions that were running through my mind. So there I was, awoken from a deep sleep, and I just swung out to hit her. My arm went right through her as if she were some sort of hologram. As my eyes focused on her body, I then noticed that her form wasn't fully there—it had a somewhat translucent look to it, almost like when Carrie Fisher did the R2-D2 holographic message from Star Wars, saying "Help me, Obi-Wan Kenobi. You're my only hope." So I was able to see through her as she slowly disappeared. I jumped up out of bed as fast as I could to turn on the overhead light, asking myself, "What just happened? Did I just see that?" as I tried to determine if I was awake. "Yes! I am awake," I said.

I checked the bedroom door. It was still locked. The window was still locked. I went out to check the front door, but it was still locked. So yes, this weird holographic moment really did happen. It would make anyone scared to go back to sleep.

I still to this day don't know why I had that encounter. I think of it as a sign, saying you are not alone—there are things in this world beyond death, things beyond our scope.

Had she been my spirit guide or someone from the other side? Or had she been some random ghost that had woken me up for a reason?

Was it something that I dreamed up? I was in a deep sleep, but when you sense someone is standing right over you and you open up your eyes to see someone standing over you, it is a bit freaky. That encounter, while unsettling, was always a good vital sign. It showed me that there is more to life after death—things that we can't explain.

Right now, to this day, I will never sleep in a fully dark room because of that. I always leave a light on. My mother once told me about a similar experience that she had. She said she was at home in bed and had awoken herself up because she was talking out loud to someone in her sleep. She said that she had opened up her eyes to see an old Indian man standing by her bedside, talking to her. So she said she re-closed her eyes again, thinking she was just dreaming, but then she realized, "No! There is someone standing right by my bedside."

She said she looked again at this Indian man, wearing the feathers and the whole Indian clothing from the olden days. He slowly disappeared right before her eyes. I'm sure she had the same response as me: "What the hell did I just see? Did this just really happen?" So maybe she got a visit from her spirit guide as well? Now, before you start saying it was just a hallucination that was brought on by lack of sleep, which does happen, this is different. I say this as a fact because I had recently had a sleep deprivation hallucination experience myself. Although it was scary, it just wasn't the same thing. I even googled it to make sure I wasn't crazy.

It seems to be a common thing that happens to people working long shifts. So I was working a lot of overtime at a call center—I was putting in 60 hours a week. All that money was going to fund my vinyl records and CDs. During this "sleep deprivation hallucination," I remember waking up confused in my room. I was in my bed, yet I would've sworn that there was this man in my room, looking right at me. Of course, I froze. You know, it's like waking up to a bunch of people looking right at you.

For one thing, you are wondering, "Who are these people? Why are they looking at me? Where am I? What is happening?" And you're probably confused at that moment. I wasn't sure what was going on.

I think this happened so fast I didn't even try to move at all. I just laid there looking at this man dressed in all white standing by the wall, wondering, "Who is that and why is he in my room?" I felt scared for a second, you know, like that shiver you get down your spine?

Well, I swear within the snap of my fingers, he was gone! As if he had morphed into the set of tall speakers that were standing right where he was in my room. Of course, I jumped up, trying to figure out, "What the hell just happened?" So, of course, I go to Google for the information. I found the answer pretty fast. Apparently, people who work long hours and have lack of sleep can get hallucinations.

This happens when you wake up while in a dream state. Your mind doesn't know that you are awake yet, so what you end up seeing is an illusion of your dream layered over real life. Within a snap of your fingers, your brain realizes that you are awake and removes the dream in just a snap; therefore, you get this morphing effect. So the speakers were the same height as the man and in the spot where I thought I saw the man.

When I reflected on it, the man I saw was the Maytag man from the washer commercials. So it makes sense now. Granted, I'm not sure why I would be seeing the Maytag man, but I had seen the commercials, so it was in my memory.

Sleep Deprivation vs. Spiritual Experiences:

I found out that what I experienced is a common side effect of sleep deprivation. When I think back to the woman I had seen in the blue dress, she didn't disappear in a snap, and she also didn't morph into anything on the spot. This was not the same experience, and I wasn't sleep deprived at the time. I believe that experience involved a spirit—not a ghost or hallucination. She faded away slowly, versus the "snap, I'm gone" approach that you mostly get from sleep deprivation.

According to Google, sleep deprivation occurs when a person doesn't get enough sleep. This can be a short-term issue affecting one or a few nights, or it can be a chronic concern lasting weeks or even months. Sleep deprivation can happen for countless reasons, many of them harmless, but it's also a key symptom of certain health conditions. Sleep deprivation can lead to hallucinations, also known as sleep deprivation illusions, where the brain misinterprets information and creates false perceptions.

These illusions can range from visual disturbances like flashes of light or shadows to hearing or feeling things that aren't there. Here's what I discovered about these two phenomena: The sudden disappearance of a hallucination and the gradual fading of a spirit are distinct experiences.

Hallucinations can vanish abruptly, often linked to a specific trigger or underlying cause, while the fading of a spirit is a more gradual process, potentially suggesting a weakening or lessening of a spiritual presence. So what do you believe? I believe one was a spirit visiting me, and the other was a sleep hallucination.

Let's talk about my other experience: As I mentioned before, as an adult, this has been very low-key. By low-key, I mean it's not in-your-face like what a psychic would typically see.

The Angel at the Blood Drive:

You would always find a way to dismiss it. "Oh, I must've been dreaming," or "I must have been sleep-deprived." You know those times when you're so tired that you start to hear "radio voices" or "people talking"? Well, then you know it's time for bed at that point.

Anyway, here are some more adventures:
In high school, I weighed 120 pounds, and the American Red Cross came to our school to collect donated blood. I decided I wanted to donate blood. The lowest weight limit was 120 pounds, so I was right at it. I remember giving blood and being proud of myself. The lady told me to lie down for a minute before I got up to walk.

Once I was done, I got up and felt fine, so I walked over to the snack table where two high school girls were sitting. They told me, "You can only take one snack from the table." As they were telling me this, I felt a very strong faint coming on. My hearing suddenly went away, and I could feel my body starting to fall.

Out of nowhere, someone caught me. I just remember it was a guy who had swooped in like a superhero, caught me, and lifted me up in his arms, giving me a strong hug. The feeling I got was interesting—like an overwhelming feeling of pure love entered my body. An almost heavenly feeling is a way to describe it.

I remember being laid down on a floor mat. At that point, my hearing was completely gone, and I remember looking up at the gym ceiling and saying to myself, "God, please, I'm not ready to die. I still need to finish school and grow up to live a full life." At that point, I realized that I wasn't ready to die.

Looking back on it, the feeling of being wrapped in those arms was a feeling of pure power—like the deepest love you could ever experience. A complete love is an experience unlike anything in this world, so I believe it was an angel who had swooped in, in a male human form, and swooped out so fast that apparently no one else saw him. Wouldn't you like to believe it was an angel and not just some random guy working for the American Red Cross?

Like I said, I looked around and never saw him, so it's impossible he could've been a worker there, right? The school called my grandparents to take me home, and I told them about my heavenly encounter.

Steve's Ghost:

My mother refused to sleep in her room after Steve died. He died in the room. Before he died, his brother, who was a priest, came up to visit with him and pray for him, making sure that he made it to the good side once he kicked the bucket, so to speak.

Mother would sleep in a twin bed in my sister's old room, which she had her mother staying in. Mother refused to sleep in her room for a full year, so she and my grandma shared a room. That is when I started hearing about strange things that were happening.

My grandma had told me that she was at home alone with the front door locked, and she had to use the restroom. She said she was sitting on the toilet and was looking at the closed bathroom door when she saw the door knob turn like someone was going to come in. So she yelled out, "I'm in here! Just a minute!" and the door knob stopped turning. She got up after doing her business on the toilet.

She said she thought that one of the grandkids may have come into the house, but she said the front door was still locked and no one else was there, so it spooked her out. Now granted, my grandma is the kind of person who would kick the dog out of the restroom.

I remember her saying, "I don't want the dog looking at me using the restroom or taking a shower." I don't blame her. I mean, I had always thought that it was weird that people would shower, use the bathroom, masturbate, or even have sex in front of their pets. It's just weird. Does your pet need to see you doing that? Privacy is a thing that we all should have completely at some point in the day.

One of the grand kids had said that she was using the toilet when all of a sudden, the water knob to the shower turned on by it's self. She ran out of the bathroom screaming.

STAFON VON CAMRON

First hand experience:

One of the grand kids had said that she was using the toilet when all of a sudden, the water knob to the shower turned on by it's self. She ran out of the bathroom screaming. My grandma said she would hear footsteps in the hall late at night when no one was there. Granted, I was being told this but I didn't really believe them, thinking of it as just random coincidences. When I finally go visit Mother I would get a first hand paranormal experience.

I was standing in the kitchen talking to my sister and my grandma, when out of no where, it seems like someone or something unseen took both hands from behind me to cover my eyes. All I could see was milky white. I was freaking out saying out loud. "I can't see, I can't see!" in a panic. I'm not hearing anything out of my grandma or sister. It's as if they were just sitting there looking at me wondering what was going on, almost like a "what should we do" kind of moment.

What seemed to go on for minutes, my vision finally came back. I was glad. Let me tell you, I was scared. I didn't know what had happened. I never had that happen to me before, so it couldn't be medical—I mean, if it was, it would have happened since, right? So I chalked it up as maybe just a rare thing; I just needed to eat something, I guessed.
Things would only get weirder after my mother, grandma, and sister left to go on a cruise, leaving me to watch after the house. I was left to babysit her house while they were gone.

Granted, this was also the time that I had been going to school to get my master instructor's license, so I was in school during the day and there at the house at night.

One night I was in my room when I heard a knock on the front door. So I went and looked to see who was knocking, but I didn't see anyone. I opened up the door and looked around. No one was there.

I then locked the door back up and went back inside. Then I thought about it afterward: "Wow, next time don't just open the door. After all, it was out in the middle of the country at night, so no one was around to help you if it was a robber or serial killer." So I thought, "Yes, please don't ever do that again!"

I go back to my room and shut the door. Then I start hearing someone walking up and down the hall. I opened my door to see who it was—no one was there. I checked the house, but there was no one. I thought, "Well, maybe I'm just hearing things." I wished that was the case.

It ended up being footsteps and doors opening and closing all night long. You would hear this happening in real-time, but when you would go investigate, the doors would all be open, even though seconds before, you would hear them slamming closed.

This finally got me thinking: Steve's ghost was still in the house; however, it wasn't in the same dimension as ours. I only decided this because I was getting the real-time noises but not seeing anything moving or seeing it physically happen in front of me. So when I heard the door close or open and went to look right away, it was always open, but I had heard it close. So remember when my grandma had seen the door knob turning, but no one was there as she used the bathroom? She was seeing a physical movement.

Theories About Steve's Presence:

Was she seeing the other realm at that moment? They say that when some people die they:

A: *Stick around to observe people until they get bored and move on.*

B: *They refuse to cross over and stay behind, for fear of being judged by God.*

C: *Don't know that they are dead, and might take a while to realize why people don't notice them or talk to them.*

D: *They depart into the bright tunnel right away, going to their real home on the other side.*

I think Steve stayed behind for a bit. This was causing the noises and the physical movements of objects at some points. One day, when my grandma was out shopping with her boyfriend, I thought that she had come home. I heard someone walking down the hallway going to her bedroom and shutting the door. Moments later, I go to her door, knock on it, and ask, "Grandma, are you there?" I got no response.

So I go back to my room, thinking maybe she took a nap or didn't hear me. About an hour later, I hear footsteps in the hallway again. I go look, and it's Grandma and her boyfriend coming home. I looked at her and said, "I thought you came home an hour ago and went to your room?"

She said, "No, I'm just now getting here. Why?" That freaked me out a little. I told her about it. She said that she often would hear footsteps too and was glad that I confirmed that she wasn't the only one to hear things going on in the house.

My mother had come home, and I was telling her about hearing footsteps walking up and down the hall and about the doors opening and closing. She seemed somewhat interested in what I was telling her.

She had been telling grandma "that she wasn't hearing anything—it was just the echo of the hall on the wooden hall floor before they laid down the carpet." So I don't think she believed her or me at the moment.

I think Steve was just playing around, trying to scare me or to let me know he was there.

****

Mother's Strange Experience:

She said that while she would shower, she would hear this buzzing sound above her head. You see, there was a storage area above the shower where Steve stored his electric toothbrush. Mother said that every time she was in the shower, it would go off, but when she would check it, there were no batteries in it. So it was impossible, right? I think she was hearing the phantom sounds, just like me and Grandma, from Steve's ghost realm.

Thinking about it, as she was telling me this, we all of a sudden heard a loud beeping sound the moment that she said Steve's name. I asked Mother, "What was that?" a little freaked out. She says, "Oh, that's just Steve's watch," and "For whatever reason, it just randomly beeps, even when the battery in it is dead." Like, how does she not put two and two together? Here is a dead watch, a dead toothbrush, and a ton of electrical items doing freaky things with no power.

If you were to ask a psychic like Sylvia Browne this question when she was alive, she would say, "Honey, that's his way of letting you know that he's still around. Ghosts tend to have a way of messing with electric currents." So this makes sense. I just wonder if ghosts can turn door knobs and turn on water faucets too.

If you saw the movie "Ghost" with Patrick Swayze and Demi Moore, I guess ghosts can use the energy around them to move things around. I personally only heard noises; I didn't see anything happen. While my grandma may have been able to see and hear the things happening.

The fact that it made noise while we were talking about him was a bit freaky. I think he was just letting us know that he was listening to us talk about him. Mother had told me that she had a dream that Steve had told her that he was going to leave her alone so she could go on about her life, so she could find a new life partner. I hear that ghosts often come to us in dreams to leave a message. Ever since then, nothing has been reported.

I stayed there a few more times and never had anything weird happen since, but I'm always uneasy going there because of the bad memories. Since then, my mother has built onto the house, so the layout has changed—bigger bedrooms built out.

On another note, when Steve died, all of the electronic items that he owned stopped working. My mother said his belongings like his TV, CD player, VCR, watch, toothbrush, DVD player, etc., all didn't work anymore.

I just thought, "Mother, maybe it was just a power surge that blew out some of those electronics." But then another part of me was like, "Yeah, I can see that. Steve wouldn't want anyone to get any use out of his stuff, so I could see him destroying them all so you couldn't use any of it."

As far as the watch and toothbrush, maybe they just had low batteries that would sometimes work for a second. Or maybe Sylvia was right—Steve was letting them know that he was still around by using some of his energy to power them on for a few seconds. I'm leaving this undecided.

Remember when I said I had never had my vision go pure white before? Well, when we found out about Cameron getting burned alive in Troy's little two-story cabin, we drove over to see the property. My sister saw guts in the fire and started to cry. She for some reason thought that they belonged to him; however, it just turned out to be from a small cat that belonged to the lady next door. I guess it would go over and hang out in the cabin with Cameron.

It didn't escape the fire. Once we were all driving back home, cramped in the back seat of mother's beat-up truck, I started feeling weird. Not only that, but I was freaking out because I felt like my eyes were trying to roll backward inside of my head, or so it felt that way. My sister is a nurse, so she said that I was probably having seizures brought on by stress. No, they didn't take me to the hospital. The drive home seemed to take forever. I suffered the whole way. The feeling lasted a good 60 minutes or so. Whatever it was, I never want to experience it again.

According to Google, eyes rolling back can be a symptom of several conditions, including fainting, seizures, or nystagmus. It can also occur during sleep or as a nonverbal communication gesture. In some cases, it can be a sign of a more serious condition, such as a stroke or brain tumor.

The most common causes include seizures, fainting spells, or an eye condition called nystagmus. Many times, your eyes rolling back and other accompanying symptoms are due to an underlying health condition. Oftentimes, your symptoms will go away when the underlying condition is treated.

Honestly, it hasn't happened since. I think at that time I was eating unhealthy fast foods, so I think it was health-related. In my "Lose Weight" chapter, I talk about how all my underlying medical conditions went away. I'm sure if you were to ask some religious fanatic, they would say "that my body was being attacked by Cameron's demon trying to find a new host body" since it was waiting for someone to feed on. Of course, that is nonsense.

I keep my body pure with God's light, so to me my condition was purely medical. Last but not least, in my quest to prove that ghosts do exist, I was going to catch one in the act. However, I didn't know I would be so embarrassed about it.

So one day, my mother and I were at a local gym where she had a membership. I was around 10. She and I were walking on the outdoor paved track that went around about a mile in a loop, so you could do as many loops as you wanted.

I told Mother that I had to use the restroom, so I ran over to the restroom that was on the other side of the track. I went in to pee and leave. Just as I walked around the corner, I heard the door open back up and close again. Granted, the door was a metal door and it wasn't easy to open, so I thought, "What if it was a ghost?" So I was going to prove that ghosts were real. If I looked fast and saw no one was in the bathroom, that would prove it, right?

However, as I ran back over to the door, I yanked it open fast, saying, "I got you!" expecting to see a ghost standing there. To my shock, I saw a surprised older man looking right back at me as he was taking a leak in the urinal that was right next to the door. Anyway, he looked up at me, spooked, as I was also spooked. I wasn't expecting it to be a human, but here I was, looking at someone in a private moment. Moreover, I was embarrassed. I ran back over to my mother, telling her about it. So when the guy walked by us and said "good morning" to my mother, I was beet red with embarrassment.

Mostly because I had burst in on this guy while he was peeing, I was unable to prove that a ghost was around that day. Another embarrassing time—as far as seeing another older man exposed—was when my friend and I went to the water park to use the restroom. Once we walked in, there was this adult male hanging out in the open in only his birthday suit. We both stood there frozen, not knowing what to do.

My friend ran out pretty quickly. I shortly followed him, but before I did, I noticed the guy had hair down there. "Wow," I thought—something that I had just newly discovered. So I told Mother about it later, saying, "The guy had hair down there!" She just laughed about it. I was just finding out that men grew hair down there too. So those are all my spirits and ghost stories. Not much, really. Just a few things that happened.

Does this prove anything?

See, it's hard to tell what is real and what your mind perceives as real. Once, a reporter asked a question to the great and late Betty White. When asked about death, she summed it up pretty well:

"My mother had a wonderful approach to death," White said. "She always thought of it as—she said, 'We know we have managed to find out almost anything that exists, but nobody knows what happens at that moment when it's over.'" She continued: "And she said, 'It's the one secret that we don't know.' So whenever we would lose somebody very close and very dear, she would always say, 'Well, now he knows the secret.' And it took the curse off of it somehow."

CHAPTER EIGHT
Losing Weight

Looking back to my high school days, I was pretty thin at only 120 pounds. Nowadays, I would say a little too thin. However, I remember my uncle Clay said, "Enjoy it because it goes away as you age." By the time I got into my mid-teens, I was 140 pounds. I found that weight, while I was slim, looked healthier on me. When I hit my twenties, I was hitting 150 pounds, so it seemed every decade I would gain 10 pounds. There were a few times I had to lose weight. The first time was easier. I had to exercise and diet for a few months to get a result.

The bad thing about going to the gym and doing 8 miles of cardio is then going to a fast food joint for a cheeseburger —all the calories you spent burning off at the gym, you just got back in just a few minutes. So I can see why dieting is hard. When I was younger, I had always been a picky eater, so much so that I would even hide food away inside the center leg of the table.

I never understood why my mother would give me food on my plate that I refused to eat. It's torture for a kid. If they don't like it, why force it on them? Years later, Mother would say, "I knew about your hiding spot inside the table." It wasn't just me doing it; my sister was too.

So for some reason, as an adult, I had gained some weight. I was 166 pounds and not happy about it, but no matter how much I worked out and dieted, it wasn't budging. Before I knew it, it crept up to 180 pounds. I then thought, "Damn, I'll take back the 166 any day." I had went to the doctor for a checkup. I was having chest pains.

The doctor did tests and said that I had very high cholesterol levels. He said I should probably work on eating healthier foods. I also got a chest scan done; they didn't find anything wrong, so it was all from poor diet. I started eating salads and drinking water, so by the time of my next appointment, my cholesterol level was normal. For some reason, I went back to eating fast food, with Taco Bell being my go-to. I would sometimes get the $5 lunch box up to 3 times a day with a large soda every time. I was getting bigger and bigger but didn't care. I was stressed out and depressed.

On a side note:

I look back now on videos of me, and I'm shocked at how big I was. I could see how much I had lost—I looked like a different person.

Losing weight at any stage is a transformation. The only bad thing about it is having to buy all new clothes. I lost a total of 60 to 65 pounds. If you lose a ton more weight than that, then you'll also have to get skin removal surgery. Also, losing weight in the face makes the wrinkles more noticeable, so getting a face filler is recommended.

The first weight to go was in my face, with my stomach taking the longest area to lose weight.

Recommendations:

So one doctor said a water fast is the best thing for your body. It removes everything that the body doesn't need, and this will clear any issues. What causes dieting to fail? We only crave food because we crave the salt, the sugar, the sweetness that we have made our bodies crave, like a drug.

The new diet:

I set out on a 3-day water fast at first, drinking nothing but water. The first day was really easy. Skipping a meal wasn't so hard. On day two, I woke up hungry but ignored it and drank water all day. On day 3, I was throwing up large amounts of salt water—it was so salty. I had heard that this is part of the body's cleaning process; it was getting rid of all the salt that it didn't need.

I decided to try for 7 days on my water fast, so I continued. I found days 4 and 5 to be easy. My hunger was gone. When I woke up on day 6, I had to run to the toilet and throw up —you guessed it—a large amount of salt water. Day 7, I woke up feeling great with no hunger at all. Stepping on the scale and seeing that I lost 10 pounds was exciting! So I said, "I'm going to keep doing the water fast for another two weeks." I found that I was no longer hungry or had any cravings for sugar or food. I was losing 10 pounds every week. I ended up staying on the water fast for 30 days straight. I was aiming for 40 days, but my mother freaked out when I told her about it and was begging me to start eating again.

Starting The Keto Diet:

I had lost a total of 40 pounds at that point. I knew that 10 pounds of it was water weight and that it would come back the moment I had something to eat. I planned out what kinds of food I would eat. I decided I was going on a keto diet, which is pretty much the same thing as the old Atkins diet—a diet that was low in carbs, high in protein and fat, with no sugars. I found it great. At first, I went overboard making all kinds of keto foods. There was a replacement for everything.

I found it great; however, it was getting pricey. So I focused on just a short list of foods: cheese, avocado, eggs, bacon, and tomatoes. Those were my go-to foods. I would eat one big plate a day, and I was good to go. One meal a day fasting. I was losing 10 pounds a month. So by the time I hit my goal of 140 pounds, it had only been 6 months. I kept the same diet and was able to stay at 140.

I did start to subtract things and add things to my meal as I went along to see what helped or made it worse. For instance, when bacon and egg prices went super high, I switched over to peanut butter. The problem was I was eating a lot of it because it's so good, so I saw my weight climbing. I had to lay off of it for a while and would buy it less and less. Once I got back to the 140 mark, I then switched over to peanuts.

This seemed to give me the protein that I needed and didn't cause me to gain. It was also cheaper than eggs and peanut butter. So I dropped eggs and bacon because of the costs and replaced peanut butter with whole peanuts. I still did my cheese, avocado, and tomatoes. Staying on a strict diet is hard, but you gotta think about when you were overweight and unhappy.

That just resets your mind, saying, "This is your new way of life." After a while, I was so bored of just drinking water, so I started buying the Zevia soda that uses the stevia leaf to sweeten it. I loved my Zevia sodas, but they were so expensive! I was buying $100 a week just in soda. So I had to find other ways.

I then switched over to water with the little flavor pods. I did that for a year while buying Zevia once a month. I found trying new things helps determine what works and what doesn't. I even tried zero-sugar sodas. They tend to be cheaper and never cause any weight gain, so I have my list of things that replace sugar but still give me a treat. I love the keto ice cream. Most candy on keto is sweetened with sugar alcohols. This means they taste like the real thing; however, you have to eat less of them if you don't want to be farting all day.

Sugar alcohols can leave you gassy or give you the runs if you have too much. So any time I'm craving chocolate or candy, I will buy sugar-free. I just have to eat less of it.

I found that eating and putting things in your body depends on you picking the right things. Being healthy is all about you sticking to less over more. Once you train your body with what it needs versus what you want, you will find this process is a lot easier. One thing I use to distract me from snacking is gum.

I chew sugar-free gum all day when I'm at work. Not only is it a great way to keep hunger at bay, sugar-free gum is also great for your teeth. Keep in mind that gum can be used to pop or blow bubbles too. Gum not only distracts you from food, it works out your mouth, neck, chin, and jaw muscles. I found before this, my jaw used to get tired. Now I can chew all day with no soreness, and it's great.

I find that everyone has a weight-loss solution that works for them. The main thing is to try to cut your food intake and eat fewer carbs. Reduce your sugar intake. Just doing those two things, you will start seeing the results. Of course, the way they label products nowadays, you gotta look at the chart. Fat-free food is a lie. They may remove the fat in the food but add in tons of sugar and carbs, which will make you fat.

****

I notice this with some sugar-free foods too. They remove the sugar, but it will have a ton of carbs. Carbohydrates turn into sugar, so even if it is sugar-free, you still are going to get sugar. As you know, sugar turns into fat in your body. I learned so much from watching weight loss videos for keto.

According to Google:

The ketogenic, or keto, diet is a low-carbohydrate, high-fat eating plan that encourages the body to burn fat for energy instead of carbohydrates. This process, called ketosis, involves the liver producing ketones, which are then used as fuel. The diet is often followed to facilitate weight loss and manage certain health conditions.

Key aspects of the keto diet:

Low-carb: Carb intake is severely restricted, usually to 20-50 grams per day.

High-fat: A significant portion of calories comes from healthy fats like olive oil, avocados, and dairy.

Moderate protein: Protein intake is moderate, with sources like meat, fish, and eggs.

Ketosis: The diet aims to induce ketosis, where the body uses fat for fuel instead of carbs.

Benefits: Potential benefits include weight loss, improved blood sugar management, and potential benefits for neurological conditions.

Foods to avoid: Carb-rich foods like grains, beans, fruits, and starchy vegetables are restricted.

Foods to eat: Animal proteins, dairy, non-starchy vegetables, healthy fats, and oils are common choices.

Note: The keto diet can have potential side effects and may not be suitable for everyone. It's crucial to consult with a healthcare professional before starting the diet, especially if you have underlying health conditions or are taking medications.

Besides being in ketosis, I find that fasting is a great thing—it keeps you focused more on your life with fewer distractions from food. Some people have a horrible relationship with food.

My mother also lost weight—maybe I inspired her through my weight loss journey. However, hers was a different approach; she used the Ozempic shot. Some people might combine the methods of weight loss.
My methods were water fasting step one and keto step two. Hers was step one, Ozempic, and step two, eat whatever.

Potential benefits:

Enhanced weight loss: Using both Ozempic and the keto diet can promote weight loss independently. Ozempic helps suppress appetite, while the keto diet encourages fat-burning. Combining these approaches could potentially lead to more significant and sustained weight loss.

Reduced cravings and hunger: Ozempic's appetite-suppressing effects can help you adhere to a calorie-restricted keto diet more easily.

The point of a diet is to lose weight, but you have to be willing to stick to it for the rest of your life. Like Dolly Parton once said, "A little bit of this and a little bit of that is all you need."

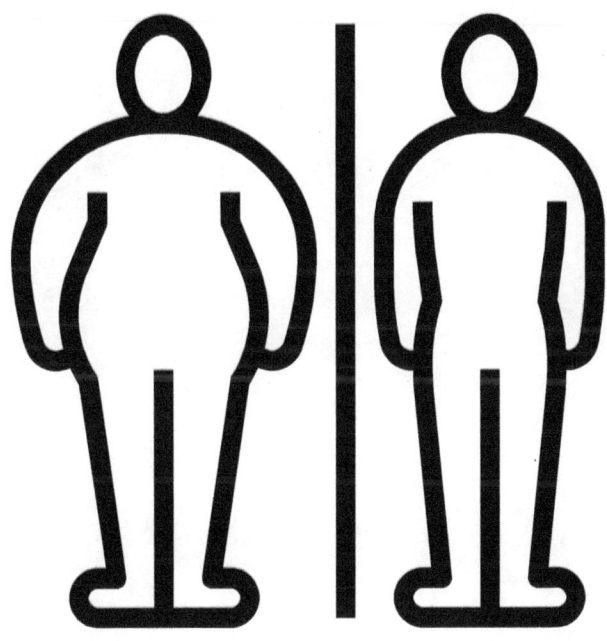

CHAPTER NINE
Memories Of Life

Insecurity:

One of the things that I have to struggle with is my speaking voice. People will say I'm very soft-spoken. My speaking voice is high-pitched and soft. It doesn't project well. I figure that might be a gift since I'm able to sing a bit higher than most guys, but I'm still able to sing lower, too. I'm always wondering if people are judging me based on my talking voice. It has never been deep. And on the phone, I get called "Miss" or "Misses" a lot.

It got to the point where I stopped correcting people because I got so tired of trying to explain that I am Mr. Von Cameron and not Mrs. Von Cameron. There is no Mrs. Or they/them. The only other person I can think of that had a higher, child-like tone to his voice was Michael Jackson.

Apparently, there is a spectrum. According to Wikipedia, male voices are generally characterized by lower speaking pitches compared to female voices, typically ranging from 90 to 155 Hz. This range is roughly an octave lower than the average female speaking frequency of 165 to 255 Hz according to Wikipedia.

As men age, their voices may become slightly higher, but this is a relatively small change compared to the overall difference between male and female voices.

While the overall speaking pitch of a male voice is lower, there are variations within male voice types: countertenor, tenor, baritone, and bass.

****

Countertenor: The highest male voice type, often with a range similar to a female contralto.

Tenor: A mid-range male voice type commonly used in operatic performances.

Baritone: A midrange male voice type often described as the most common male voice type.

Bass: The lowest male voice type, typically ranges from F2 to E4.

If I were to guess my singing voice, I'm a countertenor. Countertenors need to be able to access and control a very high range using falsetto, a vocal technique that is not naturally possessed by most men. I always just called it a "throat voice."

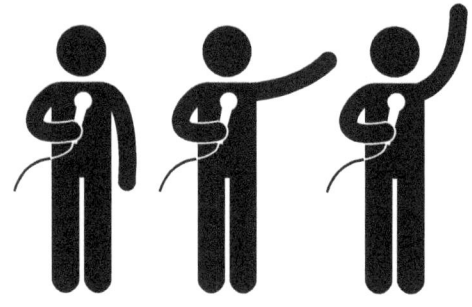

School Bus Ride:

My sister and I used to stand at the end of the driveway, waiting for the school bus to pick us up. We were on the second stop along the way. It would be freezing outside in the winter.

One day we got on the bus, and my sister sat on the seat opposite me, when a guy named Frankie happened to notice something that wasn't right. He pointed it out to my sister, and she was so embarrassed. My sister must have been so much in a hurry from getting dressed to catch the school bus that she had somehow forgotten to put both legs into her panties.

So there she sat on the bus, with her panties resting on one leg just above her shoe. When Frankie pointed at it and told her, she thought she was going to melt into the seat. She was so embarrassed.

I thought it was funny, but it wasn't that big of a deal for me. I honestly don't think Frankie cared either, as he had a sister too, around the same age as my sister. Anytime I bring that memory up to my sister, she flat-out refuses that it happened. Apparently, it was so embarrassing for her that she mentally blocked it from her memory.

Childhood Memories:

One day, back in the old childhood trailer that I grew up in, I was sleeping, and I remember this horrible nightmare that I had. I was playing outside, and some lady approached me. For some reason, she was planning on kidnapping me.

I remember running away from her around to the back side of the trailer, trying to get away. Next to our trailer, there was a tree. I ran under the tree to the front end side of the trailer, only to be blocked in by a fence. I remember climbing up the fence and trying to jump over it, but the lady was right behind me and caught up to me, pulling me down, and then I woke up. For some reason, it was a scary dream.

The fact that I remember it today shows that. I'm not sure why I had it. Our trailer never had a fence blocking it in, so I'm not sure what the dream was trying to say. So for a while, I thought my mother might have been the kidnapper. Can you imagine finding out now that you were kidnapped and the person you called mother for all of your life wasn't your real mother at all, but the woman who kidnapped you? Yeah, me neither.

The Underwear Connection:

There was one day my mother said to me and my sister, "Hurry up, brats. We are going to Walmart." We both ran out to the car, getting ready to leave, until I noticed—OMG, I had forgotten to put on pants. I was wearing a shirt, jacket, shoes, and only underwear. So of course I'm like, "I need to go put on pants." And my mother laughed. Good thing I didn't go into Walmart like that.

Not sure my sister or mother even noticed. I was the one to notice at first. So when you're rushing to get dressed in a hurry, I can now see why my sister had her one-leg panty issue.

Bad babysitters:

One time at the lake, I didn't know how to swim. I was with Donna and her horrible sister, who let me get in the water. I didn't know how to swim. I remember sinking below the water. I remember looking for fish.

I also remember not being able to get back to the surface. I was young and didn't know how to swim, so I imagine that I was scared. I'm not sure who got me out. It must have been Donna. I knew that I would have drowned for sure had I stayed under any longer. I have a memory of them smoking cigarettes at a young age. They definitely were doing everything under the sun that they shouldn't have been doing at their ages. I think that's why I never got into smoking.

Fireworks gone wrong:

It was the 4th of July. We were outside the house. Fireworks were going off. A bottle rocket somehow landed in a bag of bottle rockets, and they were shooting everywhere. People had to duck behind their cars for protection. I remember ducking behind a paper bag. A bottle rocket hit it but was stopped in its tracks, and the paper bag started to light up on fire. I got lucky that I wasn't hit by it.

Burned hand:

One day, I had burned my hand, so Grandma gave me a cup of cold water. I stuck my hand in the glass to stop the pain. Apparently, my Aunt Lisa didn't know that I had burned my hand and told me to get my hand out of the glass, only to have me start screaming bloody murder as the pain returned. I think my grandma informed her about it as she told me to put my hand back in the glass cup.

Bad Mother:

One day, my mother was in the bathroom of my childhood trailer. She was standing looking in the bathroom mirror, curling her hair with a curling iron. So I asked her a question about the birthmark on my leg. At the time, I didn't know that it was a birthmark. So my mother says, "Well, you wouldn't shut up as a baby, so I burned you with a curling iron."

Apparently, this didn't fly well with the doctor, and they almost took me away from my mother. She said they had to look at my birth records to see that it was an actual birthmark and not a burn caused by her. Let's just say she probably was less sarcastic around me after that.

Childhood Hernia:

I was getting out of the bathtub. I was standing on the edge of it and jumped down into the towel that my mother had spread out to wrap around me. All of a sudden, I was screaming bloody murder. I remember hurting so bad that anything that touched my body hurt.

I remember my mother taking me to the bed, and anytime she touched me, I would scream out loud. I think she got me dressed as best as she could and rushed me to the hospital. I remember them taking me into the emergency room and putting a mask on my face as the gas knocked me out.

When I jumped out of the tub and landed on the floor, I ended up with a hernia. A hernia occurs when an internal organ or tissue bulges through a weakened area in the muscle or tissue that normally holds it in place. This bulge can be a visible lump or swelling, especially in the abdomen, groin, or navel area. Hernias are often a result of a combination of muscle weakness and strain. A hernia in a small boy is a bulge or lump that appears in the groin area, scrotum, or near the belly button. It's caused by a part of the intestines or other tissues pushing through a weakness or opening in the abdominal wall. In boys, it often appears in the groin or scrotum.

So I ended up getting surgery. I remember there were these big pepperoni circles that were attached to the stitches. I, for some reason, ripped them off—something that only a child would do. I think I was healed up enough that it didn't cause any ugly scars. I guess I'm glad that they were able to fix the issue. That is something that even adults have to worry about. I remember it hurt so much that you don't want to have one.

Dog Attack:

My sister and I were outside playing when my sister went too close to my grandma's dog, who was chained up. The dog was aggressive and bit my sister in her face, tearing off a small chunk of her face. She of course was bleeding and crying, and the adults ran out to get the dog off of her. That dog had to be put down. To this day, my sister has a slight scar where the dog bit her on the cheek.

Bitten by a cousin:

I was outside playing at my grandma's house with my female cousins. We were making mud pies from the dirt. We would be taking turns riding a little three-wheel bike. I think one of my cousins was going crazy for some reason and bit me hard, leaving teeth marks on my arm. Needless to say, she got a spanking from her mother. I remember it hurt, and you could see the bite mark for a few days.

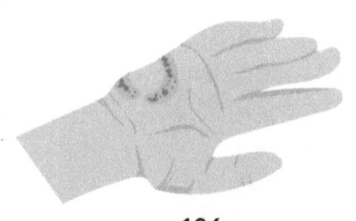

Platinum Blonde Clones:

When I was in hair school, I learned how to bleach hair well, so I bleached my hair platinum, my sister's hair, my aunt's hair, and all of her daughters' hair—all platinum blonde. If we didn't look related before, we surely looked related then. I think my sister and I were the only ones that liked the platinum color, as the cousins and their mother stuck with darker colors or highlights instead.

****

The Blue Magic Curse:

While I was in beauty school, I bought a jar of a product called Blue Magic. It said, "The original anti-breakage formula, Blue Magic Conditioner Hairdress, is formulated to give effective hair conditioning for days without being greasy, keeps hair natural and lustrous, and promotes a healthier hair and scalp condition. This moisture-resistant formula will give a special luster to your hair and help prevent dryness, breakage, and split ends." So how could it be bad for hair?

So I took it to school, and a girl there wanted me to use it on her. I put a big pile on her hair, and it was so greasy that she said even after 4 shampoos it was still greasy. So the product's claim of being "without being greasy" was a lie. It turns out the product was made for African-American hair. So if anyone of a different race used it, they were in for an unpleasantly bad surprise. I took it home and put it in my bathroom cabinet.

My sister was living in the front bedroom. Since we shared a one-bathroom trailer, she used my bathroom. I'm guessing she saw the Blue Magic and decided to put it in her hair, waiting for the miracle to happen. What she got was super greasy hair that wouldn't wash out. When she told me about it, I laughed and told her about the girl at school who had me put it in her hair. Just like me, my sister thought it was for her hair type, as it doesn't say anything about not using it on normal hair types.

Anyway, you would have thought that was the end of the Blue Magic creating unwanted magical results. Well, no—it wasn't done spreading its magic just yet. My cousin, Jennifer, who thought she could help herself to anything in my bathroom, would snoop through everything. She found a box of my blonde hair dye and decided to dye her hair without asking me if she could use it, which I did get on to her about.

Luckily, it was an inexpensive color at the time. After she had washed her hair, she was looking for a conditioner. Instead of using the one in the shower.

She spotted the jar of Blue Magic and decided to put it in her hair. When she came out of the bathroom after 3 hours, she had the most greasy-looking hair. She told my sister and me that she used the Blue Magic, and my sister and I burst out laughing. I just said, "Well, that's what you get for using stuff without asking." Anyway, it wasn't planned, so it was just funny seeing her get that instant karma. Apparently, the advertising on Blue Magic is so good that it makes all white people want to use it. After all, it's magic, right?

Well, to put an end to Blue Magic and to make sure it didn't curse anyone else with super-greasy hair, I tossed the jar in the trash. I will give Blue Magic a lot of credit for lasting so long. It went through 3 women, and still there was plenty in the jar. I was at Walmart the other day and saw a jar of Blue Magic, and it brought back this memory. So I was tempted to buy it. Now that I think about it, that would be a funny gag gift to give out at Christmas time.

Salon Business Issues:

After COVID-19 had died down, I was looking for a salon space. I had several spaces I wanted, but either they passed on a salon or the price was too expensive. I ended up getting a business partner who was in construction. He had talked me into getting a space so he could build out a salon space for me. I originally was going to rent a salon that was vacant on the second floor of the dying mall. But Danny told me, "No one will find you up here on the second floor."

So the mall manager talked us into a space on the main floor near the entry, so we would surely be seen by foot traffic. Danny hired a guy to strip the whole thing. It was left a shell. I was waiting for him to start the build-out, and he never did. I think he was only doing this so his wife could have a place to do her spray tanning service as well, but she was now asking for a divorce from him.

So of course Danny checked out his whole life on me. I was scared of getting sued for not paying the lease off. So I paid them $10,000 of my own money and never got to open up at all. Danny had got me into a pickle, talked me into his idea, and didn't even follow through with it.

I could have had the salon upstairs and started right away. Anyway, I guess God had other plans for me. After getting strung along by Danny, he convinced me that he still wanted to open up a salon, but not at the mall—at a storefront instead. So I went to scout out locations.

I found one I loved and submitted my plans to the owners. Apparently, they said they didn't want another salon since the building they owned next door already had one. I was forced to go look at another building. I found what appeared to be the perfect salon, but it was inside an office building.

Danny didn't seem too fond of that, but the color and everything in the salon was perfectly my style and taste. I tried getting the space and was about to, but someone bought the building and was planning on ripping out all of the spaces, including the salon, so I lost that salon space even before I could get it. So at this point, that was 3 spaces that didn't work out. I then found a space in the nicer part of Tulsa. The owner was nice and wanted to work with me on the price, and we went over my ideas. He was all on board until I mentioned having a huge fish tank wall. I guess he wasn't sure about that.

After not hearing back from him, I was about to just give up on the whole thing. I had already given up on Danny's worthless ass since he was useless and seemed like a talker rather than a doer. It was then that I ran into a salon that was going out of business. However, when I talked to the owner about it, she said the Christian bookstore next door wanted it so they could make it a storage room for all their inventory of books. I was like, "Who reads books anymore? Most people want audiobooks."

Anyway, she said they offered to pay her more in rent, so the space that was already plumbed out to be a salon was now being turned into a worthless storage room for books. I was secretly hoping that the bookstore would go out of business for stealing my salon opportunity away from me. I was really about to give up on getting a salon completely after looking at 5 spaces and getting nowhere.

But then, on the sixth try, I got one. This older lady had a salon that she was closing. She had been there for 30 years in total. She said it had put her kids through college, and that she was retiring and wanted to close it down. She was renting the space. It wasn't on the best side of town, but it wasn't on the worst side either—kind of in the middle of bad and good, but with some of the bad parts touching it.
I spoke with the owner, and he approved me for the space right before he died from COVID-19. The rent was half the price of a lot of other buildings, and it was already plumbed to be a salon.

My mother was out of state, but I sent her a video link to see the space. I could see what I wanted to do to it with 3D layouts. It was going to be stunning. Of course, I had to scale back my design plans from the mall space, but I had pretty much all the same ideas. So I signed the lease.

It was January of 2022. I finally had my storefront salon. It needed a makeover, though. I had to wait for Mother and her man to get back home so they could help me strip the place down. We removed the flooring, all of the carpet, the wallpaper, the stations, the mirrors—everything had to go.

I wanted everything new and modern. However, we did keep the cabinets and countertops and the front desk. We just modified the stuff. New paint, a new floor, new salon furniture, a new toilet, new hair sinks, new ceiling lighting. It pretty much went from the dull '80s salon to a modern art deco old Hollywood look—simply stunning.

The thing that took the longest to do was the epoxy floor. I wanted it to be shiny mirror black. I had my mother do the floor over and over. She had never worked with epoxy before, but she's a fast learner. The first epoxy bubbled up a lot, so it took several tries to work out all of the flaws. Once we switched over to a different product, it got way better.

We ended up going over the floor around 5 times in total. They had to sand it, sweep it, and mop it over and over and over again until I was satisfied. What started as $300 in epoxy ended up costing me $5,000 once it was done. I kept having to buy more epoxy, as I wanted a flawless floor. I came to learn there is no such thing as the perfect floor. Anyway, the salon turned out stunning, and I was so proud of it. I'm not sure how long I will have it open, but it's been open since May 2022.

I'm not sure if I'll be here for 30 years like the last lady, but I am getting the full use out of my floor. When it's waxed, it's like a black mirror. I picked black mostly to hide all of the hair. If I had my other choice, I would have done an all-glossy white—that would be horrible for a salon, but it might look super nice in a home with no kids. I think black and white are so pretty. I have my regular clients, and I get new clients every month.

So it has been great so far. I have been able to maintain a five-star status with good work and good word of mouth. I still work on music and projects on the side, so I'm living out my dream even now. I never thought about owning my own salon business before. It was only a dream, but here I am with a salon, a few albums, and now a book. So you never know what you'll end up doing in life, as it's always a surprise. It's good to set goals, but it's fun not knowing the outcome until it happens. If you don't like the results, there is always time to do it all over again. I've learned to never give up.

CHAPTER TEN
Holiday's And Pets

As kids, holidays were always the best times. I remember waking up at my grandma's house to a big Easter basket next to me, filled with candy, toys, chocolate eggs, and plastic eggs filled with money or more candy. All of us kids loved it. The Easter Bunny had come after all. And no, I don't mean on Mommy. The Easter Bunny for us was half human, half bunny that would travel from town to town handing out baskets of candy. We used to watch videos in school about the Easter Bunny, and it depicted him as similar to Frosty.

So of course, as a kid, my sister and cousins and I were all brought up to believe in Santa Clause and the Easter Bunny.

Santa Clause:

We would hear on the radio that Santa's sleigh was spotted in the sky and was heading this way. As a kid, it was amazing. Santa Clause is coming tonight. And no, I don't mean on Mommy.

So no matter how long my sister and I tried staying up to meet Santa, we always passed out, only to run into the living room in the morning to find our presents under the Christmas tree. We would both run to Mother's bedroom, excited, waking her up. She would yawn and say, "Give Mommy a minute," as she needed to get some coffee first to wake up.

The joy you felt at that moment was young, innocent, and I guess harmless—believing that Santa was real. I'm sure our mother was enjoying those times, that is, until we started public school. This was only spoiled in school when someone would break the news that there was no Santa, only because their parents didn't raise them to believe in Santa. This is not cool in a way. What's the harm in giving a child something to be excited about?

Anyway, your kid should stop spoiling other kids' holiday fun. Of course, once you found out it was your parents leaving the gifts, you had someone to blame if you didn't get what you wanted for Christmas after that. During Easter, at my mother's, we would wake up and find a box next to our beds with a cute bunny.

I loved my bunny. For a while, I kept it in my room, and it would sleep in my bed with me. However, Mother said I might roll over the bunny in my sleep and hurt it, so the bunnies went outside in a cage. When my sister and I came home from school to feed our bunnies, to our horror, we found them dead. Something wild and hungry managed to kill our bunnies. Mother thinks it was a fox or something that managed to get hold of the bunnies, as all that was left was some bloody fur.

Also, around springtime, Mother would take us to the feed store where they always had baby chickens for Easter that were dyed many bright Easter colors, looking so cute and adorable. So, of course, we ended up taking some home. We would have them in a box with a towel and a spotlight on them to keep them warm. They would all grow up pretty fast. We learned that chickens poop everywhere, and they don't care about walking in it, so they are not made to be indoors.

For a while, we had horses, pigs, cows, chickens, and a mean rooster that would chase people around. It had Tana running and screaming, as the rooster would run after her pecking at her legs, so if you've seen the movie The Birds by Alfred Hitchcock, that is what it reminded me of. All the kids would love having the rooster run after them. They found it funny but also weren't laughing when he attacked them.

For some reason, kids love taunting a brave rooster who has his pecking beak ready to peck at anyone in his territory. The rooster got attacked by one of our unknown neighbor's dogs. I remember trying to get the dog off of the rooster. He had torn off a large chunk of feathers. He must have been embarrassed, as the hens watched and heard him getting attacked. Isn't it weird that I would protect such a mean rooster? I guess the dog was going to kill the rooster, so I helped save it. That poor rooster stayed inside the shed after that. It made sure there wasn't a stray dog around before he would come back out.

STAFON AND HIS MOTHER SUSAN. (2003)

We also were on the lookout for any stray dogs coming around. I think Steve would even shoot at them if they dared step foot on our land. In the city, you would get a fine for letting your dog roam around like that.

The Pig:

We had a pig at one time. It loved to eat leftover food and loved being in a mud pit. I remember it loved to make snorting noises and was always lying out in the shade.
It had a pretty simple life, but of course, being out in the country, there were animal killers all around.

Steve was getting the pig nice and fat. I'm not sure if he was going to sell it off for money or meat, but he was mad when a stray dog attacked the pig. Unfortunately, that dog did so much damage that the pig died from the attack.

Steve was so pissed off that he went inside the house, got out the shotgun, and shot the dog on the spot. Did the pig deserve to die from a dog? No. Will a dog lover also be mad about it? If you are upset that he killed a dog, then why not be upset that the dog killed a pig? One life of a pig isn't more valuable than the other life of a dog. If you feel sad for the dog and not the pig, then something is wrong with you. Anyway, that was the only pig we had.

The poor thing got his life cut short by a dog, but the dog had its life cut short for trespassing and murdering the pig. If they had a murder trial for the dog, he would have been booked for domestic battery, trespassing with attempted murder. Since the pig died, the dog probably would have also been charged with murder in the second degree. Unfortunately, judge Steve gave him the instant death penalty.

The Goose From Hell:

We also had a goose that would chase you as the rooster did, but he was even worse. He had a big beak that would grab a much bigger mouthful of your body to pinch you with. That goose chased anyone who would step foot in the yard. What's scary is that the goose knew when we were coming home from school—as we would get off the school bus, the goose would be right there waiting for us, as if he had been waiting all day for that moment. It would chase us to the front door,

Always catching my sister to munch on. I'm sure she was as sweet as he thought she was.

My sister was in fear the whole time we had that goose. I just learned how to keep it away from me. Anytime that goose came near you, you would just kick it away from you. After a while, it knew not to mess with you. Tana, of course, never learned that trick, so she got chased by it every day. My grandma and cousins, or just anyone coming over, would stay in their cars, as the goose would attack them once they stepped out. They would be like, "Is that damned goose around?"

They always looked around to see if the coast was clear before stepping out of their car, only to be jumped by the goose moments later as the goose was hiding behind their car waiting to jump them. If they were his prey, that would be a good meal for the goose. It was kind of funny in a way. No need for a guard dog when you have a dangerous guard goose around. We started with two small geese, a male and a female. Unfortunately, the other one didn't make it, so he grew up without a partner.

The goose's ego got so boosted that it started chasing cars and trucks, thinking it was the big man on the property. One day, the goose chased a car that was driving on the road in front of our house. The goose got run over. It died shortly after that from internal organ damage. The poor thing. It was sad. Even if the goose was mean, it was still a beautiful animal that brought some people joy and some unsuspecting horror.

****

The Itches:

Besides ticks and mosquitoes, you also had to worry about chiggers and poison ivy, sumac, and poison oak. I was always allergic to poison ivy, as I had gotten it in my eyes as a baby. My sister, on the other hand, thought that she wasn't. That was until she had come to visit some land that I had bought by the lake. They came over to help clear it up with her kids. They all wore shorts. They were walking through it and even sitting near it. They all got poison ivy, even my sister.

She said it got up her legs and found all her hiding spots, including her V-A-Jay-Jay, if you catch my drift. Now she knows to stay away from it. They were all miserable for weeks. Thank goodness I didn't get it. Even one mosquito bite will make me itch for a month. I guess I'm super sensitive to any bites.

One thing that I'm scared of are snakes that bite. I was at the lake taking a look at the dock, only to notice a copperhead snake right by my foot. I jumped back fast and got out of there. Thank goodness it was cold, as it was trying to get warm on the rock by the dock. The Eastern Copperhead, also known simply as the Copperhead, is a widespread species of venomous snake, a pit viper, endemic to eastern North America. It is a member of the subfamily Crotalinae in the family Viperidae.

****

The Hero And The Snake:

One day I was at Mother's going to get some chicken eggs when I saw a copperhead snake trying to make its way inside the chicken coop. I shut the door on its tail, trapping it from going fully inside. I think he was after the chicken eggs. Anyway, he was sticking his head out at me and hissing, showing its large fangs. I knew how dangerous that snake was. If I moved my foot, it would be free to attack my leg. Next to the door, there was a shovel, so I was able to reach it. My plan at that moment was to take the shovel and cut the snake's head off.

I was shaking with fear, but I had to kill it or I would get bitten. So when the snake would stick its head around the corner of the door to show its fangs, I was going to strike at it. That moment arrived as he looked around the corner of the door—I took the shovel and BAM! I managed to chop the sucker's head off.

I was shaking. Wow, I thought. I just did something so dangerous, but also very brave. So, I gathered the snake up on the shovel and took it over to show my sister and her husband the deadly snake I killed. They seemed impressed. Those snakes can kill you with just one bite.

****

The Turkey Ostrich:

One day we were outside playing when all of a sudden we heard this weird bird sound, almost like a honking car. All of a sudden we heard our mother yell out, "Kids, don't move!" Then we saw this big turkey or wild-looking ostrich running around the yard. It also looked like a roadrunner —"Meep Meep" from the Looney Tunes cartoon. For some reason, it had come out of the woods. I'm guessing something was hunting it.

I remember it was tall, like 6 feet tall. It made its getaway back into the woods. If you can guess, Mother and Steve wanted to hunt it for some odd reason. I guess they were craving wild turkey. Well, the good news for the turkey was that it had gotten away, and they never found it again. To this day, that was the only wild turkey sighting seen there.

Pets:

Growing up, we had plenty of pets, including guinea pigs. At one point, we had fish and birds. Seems like all of them would still be around, but they all died off at some point. When I was on my own, I got a fish tank—3 of them. I had them all in a row so it looked like a huge tank. I think this inspired Mother to get a tank and fish. She, of course, went with saltwater fish, while I stayed with freshwater fish. I had a bunch of tetra fish in one tank, I think about a hundred of them. It only took one of them getting sick, and it killed them all. I learned that little fish die off way too fast, so I switched over to bigger, hardy fish.

One of my clients gave me a bunch of black and white striped fish called convicts, who turned out to be the thugs of fish. Well, they killed off all my other fish and each other. As of today, I only have one last remaining convict. He bullied his tank mate, which was twice his size—a beautiful Oscar, which was like a puppy dog. The Oscar was so excited to see you. I think Oscar fish are great. Anyway, the damn thug fish bullied my Oscar to death, so now he has the tank all to himself. If I ever get fish again, I know which ones to avoid now.

Beloved Kitten:

One time our cat had kittens. One kitten stood out. It had super white fur and these bright, stunning blue eyes. You could tell this kitten was going to be a stunning white-furred cat. Mother and Tana adored that cat so much. One day Steve's boss, Larry, came over. The stunning young cat jumped up on his tire to take a nap.

When Larry backed up his truck, the cat rolled with the wheel, getting run over. The poor thing didn't survive long after that. Mother and Tana both were crying so much over it. The beautiful cat was suffering, as there was nothing we could do to save it. They even buried it in a shoe box. That was the first time I had seen that done before.

Death Of A Pet Bird:

Granted, I cried over my bird dying. I had caught this baby bird and kept it in my room. I would feed it worms and stuff. It would cry out all the time for food. I guess I couldn't keep up with his food demands, and one day I came home from school, and it was dead. I cried so much that day. My beloved bird was dead. I would let him fly around the room, but I guess he would have been better off outside in the wild. It wasn't a newborn baby bird, just a small bird that could fly.

I remember when we lived back at the trailer, I found a small bird with a bad wing. I was able to catch it pretty easily. Mother had put it in a jar with holes in the lid. I guess she left the lid on too loose because our cat at the time, Callie, found its way into the jar and ate the baby bird. I was so mad. Bad cat, or come to think of it, bad mother. She probably left the lid loose on purpose so the cat could eat the bird. I'm assuming the bird's mother pushed it out of the nest, and it still didn't know how to fly. So it was in the grass when I found it. The bird had all of its feathers, and I was shocked at how I was able to just pick it up. Anyway, I guess you can say I love birds. Mother had bought some pet store birds.

They would fly around inside, sometimes taking them outside of their cage. But one day they were able to escape when they got out the front door as someone opened it to come inside. As they came in, the birds flew out. I'm not sure pet store birds are meant to be freed outdoors. I'm sure those birds saw that as their opportunity to be free. Even though it was a dangerous world, they didn't think there would be predators and they would end up as the next meal.

Granted, as an adult, I decided to get no birds. Why? Well, for one, they make chirping noises all day long. I can't have that. I know at night if you cover their cage with a cover, they will go to sleep. But then I think about having to clean up after their poop and the mess. Yeah, I can see why having a pet is a lot of work, so that is why I picked fish, but even they require tank cleaning and feeding.

Fish at least bring some peace to your environment and give you a beautiful setup to look at. They don't chirp or make noise, so they are mostly silent. They do require attention to keep the water just right and to make sure the tank is cleaned.

I can't tell you how many fish have died while I was learning how to take care of them. It's important to get the right tank mates or you're just giving another fish a dinner.

A worthy note:

My sister and I do not eat fish or seafood. It probably didn't help that our mother put live crabs in our beds once to scare us. She would say, "It's time for bed, kids." You would go lift the covers, only to find a big live crab with its big pinchers waiting to attack you. She would be laughing, asking, "What's wrong?"

This was when you could buy live crabs from Walmart. They had them in a big tank with rubber bands around their claws. All the kids would be gathered around looking at them. They would make good pets.

I think we always felt sorry for the crabs and saw them as pets and not food. I did buy some of those little freshwater crabs for my fish tank before. They are kind of adorable looking, with one claw being way bigger. The sad thing is, you can't have two males in the same tank, as they will fight, big claw to big claw. The loser would normally lose his big claw, and of course, the female crab would shun him over it. I guess those female crabs hate a loser.

CHAPTER ELEVEN
A World Of Questions

If you're a fan of theories, then maybe some of this will stand out to you, spark your interest, or make you think.

The Simulation Theory:

Some people believe that this world is a really good simulation—a school of life. Some others might even call it Hell. Have you ever noticed, while you are working, that the time just drags on? It can be an 8-hour, 10-hour, or even 12-hour work shift, but it just drags on and on, with the very last minutes seeming to be the longest minutes ever. Well, you're not alone. Some people think this world is just programmed that way so that when you are working, it takes forever to get to the end of your work day.

Have you noticed on your days off, they just seem to fly by way faster? Almost as if they are being sped up on purpose, so you have to get back to slaving your life away at work again? I think that is why people say our creator has a program of "Work, work, work, with very little free time." This would test anyone's patience. No wonder people become alcoholics and drug users.

Anything to escape this reality. You are strong-minded if you don't resort to such things, so you should give yourself a pat on the back. If for whatever reason you have used drugs or alcohol as an escape before, you can pat yourself on the back for finding your way back. Life is hard because it's meant to be. If you think of Earth as one of the hardest schools to graduate from, you are a great student passing the class with full A's.

This Is A School:

Some believe that this is a school. We are here to learn for God and to learn about what it's like to live a hard life in someone else's shoes. For instance, if you were racist in one life, you would have to live a full life as the race that you hated—same about gender, sexual preference, religion, appearance, disability, etc. If you do believe in heaven, how do you think everyone gets along? It's because they have walked in your shoes before.

If you've done and been everything, there is no such thing as hate in your heart on the other side.

Heaven Or Hell:

Some Christians believe that their God is the true God and that their faith is the only true faith. If you were to ask the millions of religions before that, they wouldn't agree. So, who's to even say that your religion now is even the real one?

Most Christians will also tell you that you only get one life to live. If you sin, you will go to hell. I find it odd that they preach this, but yet those people seem to be the biggest sinners of all. Also, think about it.

One life is too short, even if you only live to be one hundred years old. If you go by their "one life theory," you would be so dumb, even if you did make it to heaven. The people living in heaven are very wise for a reason. They have had several lives. The longer you are around and the more lives you have, the more knowledgeable and wiser you become.

Think about it. If you were to ask a wise person who believes in reincarnation, they will tell you that you will live many lives. If you were to ask a spiritual person, they will tell you that this is hell and that we will finally graduate once we achieve the things that we must learn, as death is our graduation or birth, so to speak. Birth is just our introduction to a long learning course that we call "Earth." Some people call this a personal hell.

Why This Is Hell:

If you think about it, no matter how much wealth you have, no matter how much fame you have, no matter how perfect your body or looks are, you will start to see the same destructive patterns. People are never happy. You get your moments of happiness, of course, but you also get pain, heartbreak, backstabbing, etc. The most successful people aren't even happy. Underneath their perfect-looking life, there is stress, worry, fears, heartbreak, insecurities, addictions, secrets, scars, etc.

So when you hear someone say, "I wish I was her or him, because they seem to have a perfect life," that isn't true at all. Taylor Swift may have all the fame and money and fans, but look at how many relationships she has been through—probably more than most women will ever have in a lifetime. If you got everything in this world, you would start to get bored, right?

Imagine that you had all the money in the world like Elon Musk. Do you see Elon spending a lot of money just for the fun of it? No, he is always working and creating because he would get bored real fast.

Fame addiction:

Some famous people get addicted to fame as if it's a drug. They love the attention, wealth, and all the things that come with it. Some people I think about who are addicted are Madonna, Cher, Taylor Swift, and many more. If they weren't, they would've retired after making all their millions and billions. Let's face it: If you had a billion dollars, wouldn't you just retire and stay out of the spotlight to live a nice life?

These women just can't do that. They have been bitten by the fame bug. Granted, I believe they also enjoy the stuff that they do. Creating art through acting and music is fun, and if you get all the benefits from that, I can see why they got addicted to fame. Some people that have all the fame but still seem humble are Dolly Parton, Kelly Clarkson, and Reba McEntire, just to name a few. Then you have the ones who got the fame, got tired of it, and walked away.

Addictions:

All of the following are addictions: money, drugs, fame, vanity, and lust. Most people are guilty of at least one or more of these. You would have to overturn a stone to find someone who hasn't. The most popular one is money. To me, the root of all evil is money. This can turn people into heartless, ruthless, selfish savages.

Of course, there are the deeper things that are more reserved for serial killers and cannibals, who have addictions that are pure evil and really shouldn't exist, but yet they do.

If you think about it. Everything we know is taught, but who's to say that any of it is correct? For all we know, our world could just be a speck of dirt on a leaf that's rotting on a sidewalk in another universe where giant people live and work.

Life as an end:

Can you imagine if you died right now—would you even have a conscience? Would you have any knowledge? Would you have any memories? Would you be able to even see anything at all? This would mean not seeing even blackness. Can you imagine that your existence is nothing? The answer is no. Since we have all experienced life, we will always want life. Have you ever seen a helpless bug in a life-or-death situation?

More Addictions:

They still are fighting to live even in their last moments. Death is scary, and that is why so many people seem to latch on to faith and religion. After all, what's the harm in believing in something if it gives you hope and relaxes your fears? Although deep down, people are scared to death. This, of course, includes dying. I've been there, and even I wasn't ready to go.

As a kid, I remember being in the back of the car thinking about what would happen after death. I remember this thought even before I even knew what church was and anything about religion. I remember I was sad about the fact that it would all be over, like I was never here. As an adult, I think that we aren't here just to be here—that would be a cruel joke to create us just to end us.

I believe that is why the Bible and other religions help give people hope, as thinking of not having anything after death is like you were never anything at all but just energy. If you know about energy, then you know it can never be destroyed.

Some people say we are part of the divine energy that is from God. So, if God has always existed, then so have we.

Spirituality Over Religion:
My Journey from Faith to Truth

My research has led me to understand even more about the universe and the reason why people are never satisfied with the life that we pick—the struggles that bear down on us. The reason why, as I've said countless times before, is because Earth is a school for us to learn for God. Not only is it a school, it can be considered living out a life to advance to the higher levels of Heaven.

According to Dolores, Sylvia, and countless others, there is no such thing as hell or the devil. That was made up by the church at the time to spread fear so they could control people. It was a form of brainwashing people. So if you sinned, you were told you are going to hell—which was called Sheol back in those days.

Think about it. Why would a loving God throw us in a furnace over something so humanized? We are told God is all loving, all knowing, but then you hear God is hateful, vengeful, and spiteful at you and will send you to hell. That kind of "you sinned so you're going to hell" talk was made up by the church to control people. They had to make a fearful God in order to get people to adopt that belief.

When someone says you are going to hell, all you have to say is you are already in it. After all, Earth is hell. This is the fake world that we are in. The other side is the real world. We are stuck here until we live out our charts. We write down when we are going to die and how we are going to die, but just like any order, you never know when it's going to show up. So as long as you do good, learn for God, and help others, you can go home to the other side.

Another thing I now believe is there is no devil, no demons —just evil beings called dark entities. These can be anyone in your family. You can usually tell one from a normal person just by a feeling alone. Does this mean anyone you don't like is a dark entity?

No, it doesn't mean that. However, the ones that are will drain the energy right out of you, making you go down the wrong path in life: drugs, alcohol, crime, murder, etc. Doing this only sets you on a path of having to come back to earth again and again until you get it right for God.

One way to convince you that you wrote out your life is: how do you explain moments of déjà vu? The reason why those moments seem familiar to you is because you wrote it on your chart. You are just remembering it, even though you typically wouldn't think about it until something triggers that memory. Have you had that moment where you say, "wait, this seems like this has happened to me before, this place, this moment this face"?

I didn't just take the word of one woman. During my research, I was hearing the same thing from other highly respected hypnotherapists through many past life regressions.

One of these respected author-hypnotherapists was Dolores Cannon, who has covered so many subjects that most people deem as fake or made up. When you connect the dots between so many people saying the same thing or sharing similar stories, it can't be made up. There has to be a logical reason they are all having the same experiences.

When you die, you see a bright light—a tunnel that is connected to your body by a silver thread to take you home. Hearing everything about what happens when you die and what it's like on the other side makes you not fear death anymore.

What sets spirituality apart from religion is that we seek truth rather than just believe what we don't see. Most people who are spiritual have experienced some kind of unnatural event in their life that leads them to being wide open to leaving hateful religion behind for a more spiritual, all-loving faith that spirituality gives you.

Here Are My Takes On Belief:

I believe that we chart out our lives before we come to earth. We pick out what we want to do, who our parents will be, what we look like, etc. Keep in mind everyone else who comes to earth also does the same thing. This leads to some people getting the fuzzy end of the lollipop.

If there is a room with one hundred chairs and two hundred people come in the room, only half will get one. The other half will get to stay in the room, but they have to stand.

So when you write down on your chart that you want a life like Taylor Swift, you might be one of the two hundred that wrote down the same thing, but the one who was lucky enough to get a seat is the one who gets that experience, but don't fret because you will get a lot of chances to do that in one of your other lives.

A Final Awakening:

As I bring this journey to a close, I want you to know that these pages represent more than just my story—they are an invitation to examine your own path. The transformation I've shared, from the confines of fear-based religion to the expansive embrace of spiritual truth, is available to anyone willing to question, to seek, and to remain open to possibilities beyond what we've been taught.

The research that changed my life—the voices of Sylvia Browne, Dolores Cannon, and countless others who have dared to explore the mysteries of existence—continues to unfold new understanding every day.

What I've learned is that we are not victims of circumstance, but co-creators of our experience. We are eternal beings having a temporary human adventure, learning and growing for purposes far greater than we can imagine while walking this earthly plane.

If you take nothing else from these pages, take this: you are not alone in your questioning. You are not strange for feeling that there must be more to existence than what traditional religion offers. That restlessness in your soul, that deep knowing that life extends far beyond what our physical eyes can see—trust it. Follow it. Let it guide you toward your own awakening.

****

A Final Awakening:

Remember, Earth is our school, not our prison. Every challenge you face, every moment of déjà vu you experience, every intuitive flash that makes you pause—these are reminders that you chose this path for a reason. You are exactly where you need to be, learning exactly what your soul came here to understand.

The light that awaits us all is not something to fear, but something to embrace. Death is not an ending but a homecoming. And until that time comes, we have work to do—not just for ourselves, but for the collective consciousness of humanity.

Stay curious. Stay open. Keep seeking truth over comfort, love over fear, and understanding over judgment. Your awakening ripples out into the world, touching lives you may never know you've influenced.

The journey continues, dear reader. And now, it's your turn to awaken.

With love and light,
Stafon Von Camron

"The truth will set you free, but first it will probably make you uncomfortable."

If this book has touched your life in any way, I encourage you to share this story with others who may be seeking their own spiritual awakening. We are all walking each other home.

Acknowledgments

First off I would like to thank Claude
for proof reading and making chances
for my very first hybrid-memoir autobiography book.
You were able to capture my whole story
in greater detail from my original audio book recording.
This written book will give the readers a better experience.

I would also like to delicate this book to:
My Mother Susan.
My sister Tana,
My grandma Sandra.
My aunts, uncles, cousins.

Please know that I love you all.
I hope you don't mind the truth.

This is my life story.
For anyone else upset with me,
I guess you will just have to wait
"Until You Awake".

Stafon Von Camron

About the Author

Stafon Von Camron is a multifaceted artist and entrepreneur who has dedicated his life to creative expression and spiritual exploration. Beginning his musical journey at the age of five, Stafon developed a passion for performance that led him to release his first independent album immediately after high school.

As CEO and Founder of SVC Music Industry, established in 1997, Stafon has built a successful career in the music business while maintaining his identity as a country singer and songwriter. His professional website serves as a platform where he shares his music, videos, and personal reflections through regular blog posts.

In 2023, Stafon continued his musical evolution with new album releases, demonstrating his ongoing commitment to artistic growth. However, his creative pursuits extend far beyond music. Following a profound spiritual awakening in 2012, sparked by Sylvia Browne's "Life on the Other Side," Stafon embarked on an intensive journey of metaphysical research and personal transformation.

This spiritual exploration led him to study the works of renowned past-life regression therapists and hypnotherapists, including Dolores Cannon, fundamentally changing his perspective on life, death, and human existence. His research into reincarnation, soul contracts, and the afterlife has become a defining aspect of his personal philosophy.

"Until You Awake: A Hybrid Memoir-Autobiography" represents Stafon's first foray into literary expression, combining his artistic sensibilities with his spiritual insights. In this deeply personal work, he shares his transformation from traditional religious beliefs to a more expansive spiritual understanding, offering readers a candid look at one person's journey toward enlightenment. Through his music, business ventures, and now his writing, *Stafon Von Camron* continues to inspire others to seek truth, embrace personal growth, and remain open to the profound mysteries of existence.

You have just reached the end of:
Until You Awake, A Hybrid Memoir-Autobiography.
Written By: Stafon Von Camron.

NOTE:
This is the 6x9 black and white version.

Cover Photo Design By: Stafon Von Camron.
Cover Photography: Miki Galloway.
Photography: Miki Galloway,
Other Photography: Susan Queen, Stafon Von Camron.
Illustrations: Video Express, Chat GPT Pro.
Art: Mixed, Created. edited with Canva Pro.

Released and Published in 2025.

© 2025 Stafon Von Camron. All rights reserved.
Unauthorized use is prohibited by law

www.ingramcontent.com/pod-product-compliance
Lightning Source LLC
Chambersburg PA
CBHW022015120526
44580CB00015B/107/J